THE TAO OF TUNINGS

A MAP TO THE WORLD OF ALTERNATE TUNINGS

BY MARK SHARK

ISBN 978-1-4234-3087-2

7777 W. BLUEMOUND RD. P.O. BOX 13819 MILWAUKEE, WI 53213

In Australia Contact:
Hal Leonard Australia Pty. Ltd.
4 Lentara Court
Cheltenham, Victoria, 3192 Australia
Email: ausadmin@halleonard.com.au

Visit Hal Leonard Online at
www.halleonard.com

DEDICATION

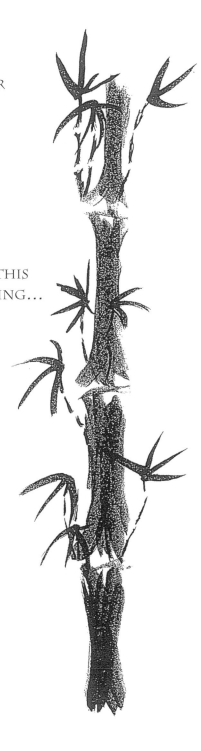

For my parents:

Mary Bray and William Schatzkamer

Both responsible for opening this
beautiful door from the beginning...

There are no words.

INTRODUCTION

Every time I pick up the guitar I am inspired by the mystery and wonder of alternate tunings. Each one is a universe of tonality where layers of sound unfold in beautiful and magical ways. The variations are infinite. The advantages of playing in tunings becomes immediately obvious when you put a slide on your finger or listen to a record by John Lee Hooker, Bonnie Raitt, Lowell George, Jackson Browne, Ben Harper, Joni Mitchell, Keola Beamer, Ry Cooder, Keith Richards, and many, many others.

It is my hope that this book will help you unlock some of the mysteries surrounding alternate tunings and facilitate your ability to take your guitar playing and musicianship to the next level. I hope they thrill and inspire you, as they have me, all these years.

Peace and happiness in discovery and knowledge,
Mark Shark
Los Angeles, California

THE TAO OF TUNINGS CD

The exercises on the accompanying CD are designed to illustrate the best way to read the fretboard diagrams, or as I like to call them, "maps." To get the most out of each map, look for the shapes that exist in a linear fashion up and down the neck on adjacent and nonadjacent strings. This will help you get the most out of each tonality. Also, look laterally (across the neck) for scale patterns and shapes that repeat from tuning to tuning. Often a combination of intervals will simply shift string groupings.

The songs on the CD are improvisational pieces that demonstrate some of the possibilities that exist in each tuning. Some of the pieces are based on songs I have written, but most are improvised in the studio. Some of the more discordant pieces were conceived while staring at one of the tuning maps and freeing myself up to explore.

I would also like to urge you to take the transcriptions with a grain of salt. It may be nice to be able to play them exactly as written, but the real treasure lies in the advantages gained by the gathering of information, ideas, and concepts. As you develop your understanding, don't hesitate to incorporate your own ideas into the mix. Exploration and experimentation is key!

ABOUT THE AUTHOR

Mark Shark was born in St. Louis, Missouri, and has been teaching, gigging, and touring from his home in southern California for the past thirty years. An accomplished musician, composer, and multi-instrumentalist, Mark's work has taken him around the world and offered him an education unique to those not attending formal studies. In his spare time he enjoys reading novels by Phillip K. Dick and Kinky Friedman, long walks with his iPod, and watching Cardinal baseball. He lives in the South Bay with his wife, two children, and a cat named Chai. This is his first book.

Further correspondence: **www.taooftunings.com**

Photo: **Dylan Schatzkamer**
Bamboo artwork: **Shiloh Schatzkamer**

Chapter 1:
SHAPES AND COLORS: PRIMARY EDUCATION FOR TUNINGS

Many people are initially hesitant to twiddle the tuning gears because doing so changes the places on the fretboard they are familiar with. It does take some getting used to, like moving to a new country and being immersed in another culture and language. However, there are parallels and relationships between different tunings, much the same as there are between languages based on Latin. The most important thing to remember is that playing in an altered tuning ultimately makes things easier.

Droning strings, convenient fingering shapes, and expanded harmonic possibilities make tunings particularly useful and beautiful. What I look for are happy accidents: convenient beauty. An impossible finger twister in regular tuning can become a simple chord progression in G tuning, for example.

To play in altered tunings you'll need a grasp of the intervallic relationships between adjacent and nonadjacent strings. One of my favorite ways to illustrate this is with tuning maps, where I provide the acceptable notes for each tonality and introduce the "spiderweb" of connecting intervals and shapes, paying special attention to thirds and sixths, as they are extremely important melodically and conceptually.

As you learn the fretboard try to envision it the way you would a piano keyboard. Find all the white keys first. Every letter-name note on every string must be instantly identifiable. Don't worry about the sharps and flats (the black keys on the piano) at first. They will become obvious once you know where the natural notes are. Learn the C major scale (the white notes of the piano). Learn how the notes of the C major scale fit together as intervals (thirds, fifths, sixths, etc.) on adjacent strings.

It's also important to be able to visualize and recognize shapes. What do thirds look like? How about sixths and octaves? Eventually you'll not only feel as comfortable playing in G tuning as you do in standard tuning, but you'll recognize the fretboard in G tuning as a more convenient way to play certain shapes and evoke deeper, more complex, sounds and tonalities.

Why Retune Your Guitar?

What is a tuning? A tuning is a fixed reference point of six tones on the guitar; four tones on the mandolin, violin, and cello; five tones on a banjo; and twelve tones on a 12-string guitar. On the guitar you have a choice of six starting points and twelve subsequent determined choices of tones.

How did standard tuning (E–A–D–G–B–E), tuned in intervals of a fourth, fourth, fourth, third, and fourth become standard? It has to do with barre chords and the ease of fingering them. If the guitar was tuned entirely in fourths (E–A–D–G–C–F), the E shape (and many other shapes) would be exceedingly difficult to finger.

For example, this barre shape: EADGBE   would look like this: EADGCF

The standard barre shape would be offline and unusable. But by lowering the top two strings a half step to B and E respectively (from C and F) the E barre shape is playable.

The same is true for the A barre shapes:

Here's a standard tuning A barre shape, with a third-fret barre:

EADGBE

Here's the same chord with the guitar tuned to fourths:

EADGCF

Obviously this shape is too cumbersome to play.

This is the primary reason standard tuning is standard. However this relationship of three fourths, a third, and a fourth puts a hitch in practicing scales. Scale patterns are no longer symmetrical, as they are on a bass (which is tuned to fourths) or a mandolin (tuned to fifths). So guitarists train themselves to compensate for the third interval between the G and B strings and become accustomed to the ensuing hitch in fingering. The advantage of easy barre-chord access in standard tuning outweighs the inconvenience of the staggered interval sequence, and once you have practiced guitar scales for a significant amount of time in standard tuning they take on graceful, if not perfectly symmetrical, shapes of their own. But they are not the only shapes that can be useful and graceful and achieve their own beautiful symmetry on the guitar neck.

Three Tunings to Start With

The first altered tuning to consider is dropped D (D–A–D–G–B–E). By simply dropping the low E string to D you expand the guitar's range and tonality. Now when you strum a D chord you can use all six strings. Of course you lose the ability to play comfortably in E and you lose the easy G chord as well. But if you want to play in the key of D, the benefits of dropped D far outweigh these inconveniences.

The second altered tuning to consider is double dropped D (D–A–D–G–B–D). This tuning lends itself to droning the high and low D strings and playing melodies on the inner four strings, particularly the G and B strings. All four inner strings are still in standard tuning, so all the usual relationships there still apply, you have just augmented your droning and tonal possibilities. You also have three open D strings and an open A string, the fifth of the D chord. This tuning is very effective for simulating the D tonality of Neil Young or Stephen Stills.

The third altered tuning to consider is open G (D–G–D–G–B–D), in which you lower the A string a whole step just as you lowered both E strings a whole step. G tuning is undoubtedly my favorite tuning on the guitar. One of the tunings used in Hawaiian slack-key, it is also infinitely useful for country, blues, rock, folk, and, of course, slide guitar styles. The first thing to consider about G tuning is that the D, G, and B strings in the middle of the guitar are still tuned normally. This gives you a great headstart toward knowing how to get around in open G. All the chord shapes in standard tuning are still present on these three important strings. Pieces of barre chords and individual triads are right where they have always been—nothing has changed. What has changed is the way you approach the other three strings. Remember that the A and both E strings have been lowered a whole step, so to regain any chord shapes you're used to, you simply need to raise the voicings on those strings a whole step. G tuning is a bit daunting at first but you now have a complete G chord in the open strings and a wonderful G bass note to drone on.

Choosing a Tuning

When choosing an alternate tuning, consider the expression of a specific tonality: major, minor, nonspecific (like D–A–D–G–A–D), or unusual (like Lydian and Locrian), as well as the ease of fingering and incorporating open strings. Choose a tuning based on what it will help you express musically and emotionally. A specific tuning will make it easier to access simple shapes that express commonly-heard motifs. When I analyze a tuning I am looking for specific shapes that represent chords or tonalities, such as the figures below:

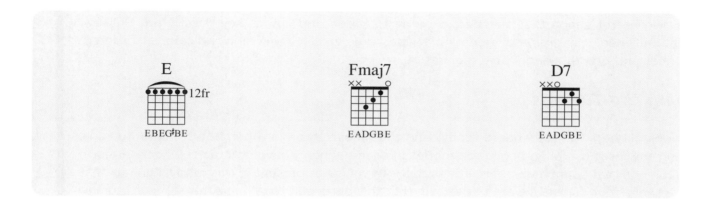

Sometimes the shape is a straight line (like the 12th fret E chord in open E). Sometimes it is a diagonal line (like the Fmaj7 in standard tuning). Sometimes it is a triangle (like the D7 chord in standard tuning). When using a slide, you want as many straight-line shapes as possible.

This book will introduce you to the spiderweb concept of viewing the neck as a series of comprehendible shapes that become predictable and categorizable when you understand the way they unfold in logical sequences.

Most music in the west involves major-scale tonality and the modes derived from it. This is the most common form of musical expression here. Major and minor pentatonic groupings of tones are also common and lay in convenient tone rows due to their simplified mathematical formula of five tones. To express these tonalities in convenient shapes it is helpful to tune to a chordal tuning, usually major, minor, or suspended. It is easiest to express major tonality in a major tuning and minor tonality in a minor tuning. Suspended tunings, such as D–A–D–G–A–D, leave the improviser more room to determine and state the major or minor tonality or leave it mystically undefined. To express more unusual tonalities it is sometimes helpful to tune to chords with flat-fives or sharp-fives so these tones can be found on open strings.

Visualizing the Major Scale

God's magic formula, the major scale, is supremely balanced. Its intervallic shapes undulate in a symmetrical fashion: two whole steps, one half step, three whole steps, one half step, repeating endlessly. On the guitar this scale can be visualized as a shape. There are eight nodes to this shape, which encompasses twelve frets. The major scale formula can be made to repeat from scale steps 1–8, 2–9, 3–10, etc., and this twelve-fret shape can be found in varying degrees on each of the six strings. It changes from key to key and string to string, depending upon the tuning selected.

When looking at all six strings, the individual shapes become part of a larger overall shape with its own pattern. This combined pattern represents six strings times twelve frets for a total of seventy-two tones. I like to view the neck in twelve-fret sections—one massive shape that repeats from frets 0–12, 1–13, 2–14, 3–15, etc. Wherever you start and end determines your key or tonality. When using a capo the key shifts up the neck depending upon where you place the capo. When viewing the neck in this way you can see that there is only one key, which always depends upon what fret you start on.

This paradigm is very useful when playing in a different key than the tuning you are in. For example, in order to access the key of A major in G tuning you would note that shape 2–14 is the exact same shape as 0–12. To play in D Mixolydian in G tuning you can shift gears and play what I call "cross guitar." Cross guitar is the same concept as cross harp, which is the method harmonica players use to play the blues on a diatonic harp. This requires you to think of the fifth step of the scale as the one. In other words, to play blues on a G harp you think of D as the root of the scale—D7 tonality. In cross guitar you use a guitar tuned to G major to play in D7 tonality. You just shift your focus on the neck from emphasizing the G as the root to the 5 (D) as the root, and shift your starting and ending points. Think 5–5 (D to D in G major), just as a harp player thinks 5–5 to access Mixolydian tones on a major-key harmonica. I view these steps of the scale as nodal points on the massive twelve-fret shape that shifts from mode to mode and key to key. This is not unlike a constellation where clusters and repeating shapes are readily found and indicate an ordered, symmetrical, and breathtakingly beautiful design.

Learning the Tunings

In this book, I'll begin with standard tuning and then move through a number of useful tunings, illustrating the most useful and common modes in each tuning. (I have omitted the Locrian mode from all tunings that contain an open fifth as this interval is not present in this mode. Tunings that contain a sharp-four or flat-five are better suited to this particular tonality.) After standard tuning I provide maps for G, E, and C tunings in their major, minor, and suspended forms. These three tunings are cousins since they share string voicings and groupings—they simply shift string groupings and bass note placement.

I'll also talk about D–A–D–G–A–D, a suspended tuning with a very open sound that is useful and familiar (the bottom four strings are the same as dropped D). Omitting the third and fourth intervals from a tuning is another way to acquire more drone notes. D–A–D–D–A–D and G–G–D–G–G–D (two root/fifth tunings) are wonderful for slide and provide great droning possibilities. And I've included certain specialty tunings for unusual tonalities, such as sharp-four tunings that open up the Lydian, Lydian flat-seven, and Locrian tonalities. E minor 11 tuning is included because it is a personal favorite of mine and David Crosby. C Wahine tuning (C–G–D–G–B–D) is a beautiful tuning that evokes a distinctively Hawaiian flavor.

When I play in any of these tunings I think in terms of root-to-root numeric values, rather than specific note names. I prefer to use numeric values within the major scale (root, second, third, fourth, etc.) rather than specific letter names of notes. This way I keep in mind the tonality scale-wise without having to be conscious of specific sharp, flat, and letter-name identifications. This helps me organize the various tunings.

All tunings have their advantages and disadvantages. Find out what a tuning lends itself to. If it doesn't do what you want it to in a simple way, there may be another tuning that does. To be sure, there's a lot to learn, and I'm gonna help you learn it, understand it, and, God willing, play it.

Chapter 2:
STANDARD AND ALTERNATE
TUNING SHAPES

Third Shapes

The guitar is a fluid landscape in which shapes shift like waves up and down the fretboard. Intervals rise, peak, and descend, ever changing, yet are fixed by theoretical gravitational forces. As you alter tunings, the shapes are altered and the intervals change in new yet utterly harmonious ways.

Examine the intervals of major and minor thirds as they rise up and down the neck in standard tuning in the key of E on the G and B strings **(Fig. A1)**.

Fig. A1 - Standard Tuning Thirds in E Major (E–F#–G#–A–B–C#–D#–E)

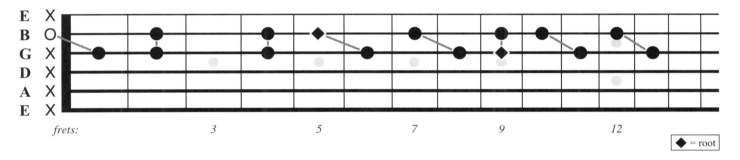

◆ = root

If you raise the G string to G# (as in open E tuning, E-B-E-G#-B-E) all the shapes change, but in a logical way. Since the G string has been raised one fret in pitch you compensate by lowering the fingering on the G string one fret in pitch **(Fig. A2)**.

Fig. A2 - E Tuning Thirds in E Major (E–F#–G#–A–B–C#–D#–E)

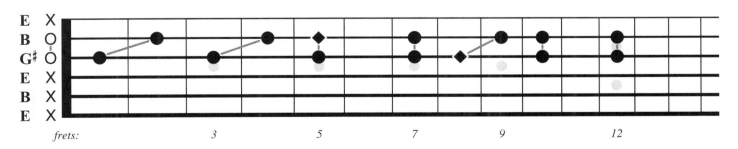

Now let's compare the relationship of the B string and the high E string in standard tuning (a fourth) to the relationship of these two strings in C tuning (a third). In C tuning (C–G–C–G–C–E) the B string is raised a half step to C. The original relationship requires the spread fingering of index-and-ring and index-and-middle fingers, to play thirds in C major on these strings **(Fig. B1)**.

Fig. B1 - Standard Tuning Thirds C Major (C–D–E–F–G–A–B–C)

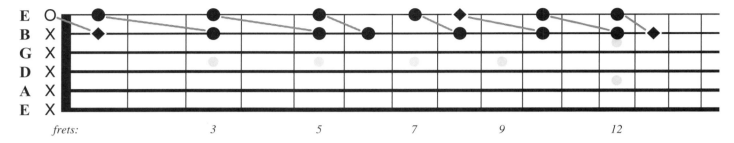

But in C tuning the shapes shift. The B string has been raised a half step, so you must compensate and lower the B-string fingering a half step. This leaves you with a smooth and balanced way of playing thirds **(Fig. B2)**.

Fig. B2 - C Tuning Thirds C Major

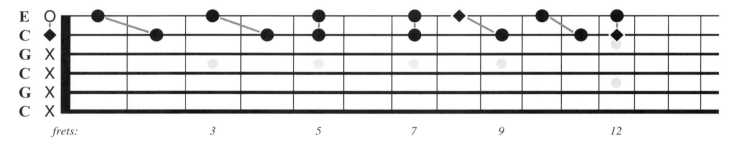

A new pattern takes shape—just as easily recognizable and logical as the original shape.

Fifth Shapes

Guitarists schooled in standard tuning may find that it takes awhile to think fluently in altered tunings. The shapes in standard tuning have become fixed in our minds and we expect the guitar to behave in a rigid and fixed way. This is advantageous in some ways. It allows us to quickly process information in a dependable fashion. However, it is also limiting, and as a guitar player, I don't want to be limited. Once you change the tuning of the guitar you have changed the canvas on which you paint intervals. Take the relationship of a fifth in standard tuning **(Fig. C1)**:

Fig. C1 - Standard Tuning Fifths in C Major

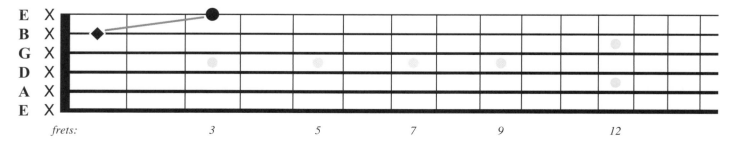

Now observe the same relationship in C tuning **(Fig. C2)**:

Fig. C2 - C Tuning Fifths in C Major

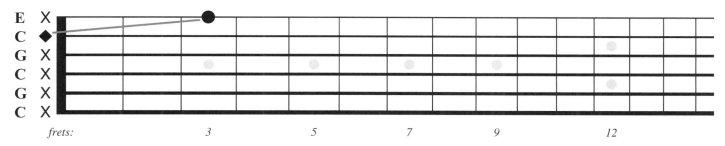

A fifth can be represented in many forms. The important thing is to recognize intervallic shapes. You'll do this by ear at first, but soon you'll memorize and categorize the patterns that intervals represent in various tunings **(Figs. C3–C8)**.

Fig. C3 - Standard Tuning Fifths in C Major

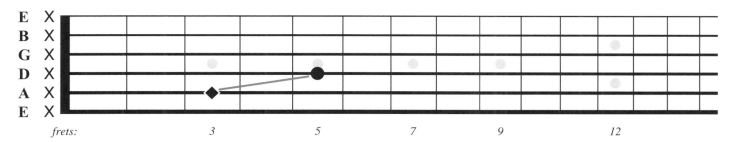

Fig. C4 - C Tuning Fifths in C Major

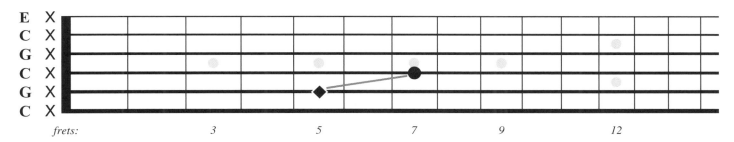

Fig. C5 - Standard Tuning Fifths in C Major

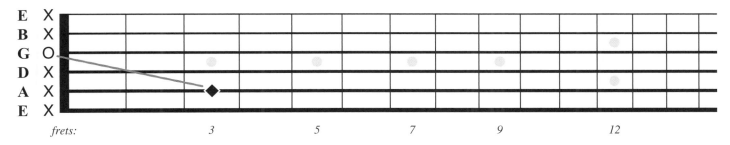

Fig. C6 - C Tuning Fifths in C Major

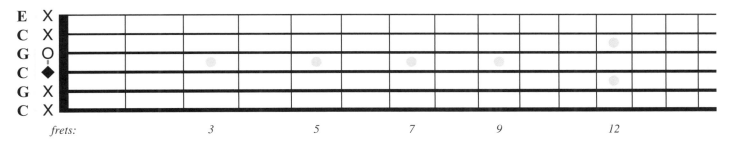

Fig. C7 - Standard Tuning
Fifths in C Major

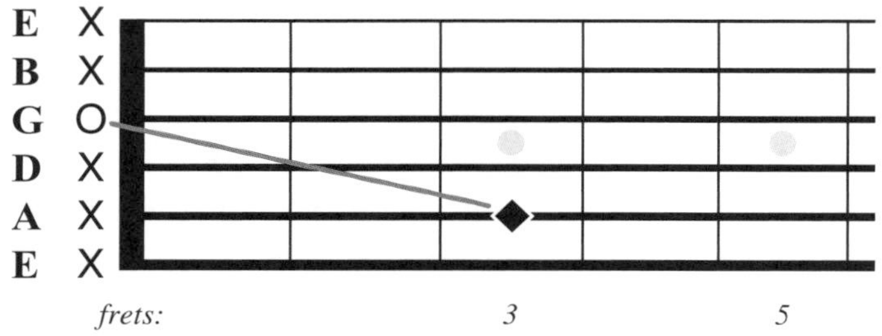

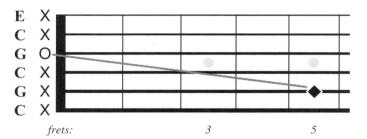

Fig. C8 - C Tuning
Fifths in C Major

Major Scale Shapes

If you compare a G major scale in standard tuning with the same scale in G tuning (D–G–D–G–B–D) you will notice some shifts. You have to use the fifth fret of the fifth string in G tuning to access the fourth (C). Also the initial root (G) has shifted from the low sixth string to the open fifth string, which has been retuned to G (**Figs. D1** and **D2**).

Fig. D1 - Standard Tuning
G Major (G–A–B–C–D–E–F#–G)

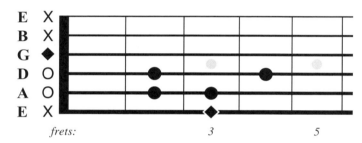

Fig. D2 - G Tuning
G Major

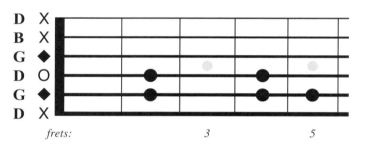

The low G–C interval has shape shifted (**Figs. E1** and **E2**), yet it remains the same when shifted up two frets on the same strings (**Figs. E3** and **E4**). The E and A strings have been lowered a whole step so you must compensate by fingering them a whole step higher.

Fig. E1 - Standard Tuning
Fourth G–C

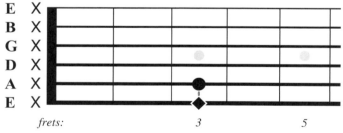

Fig. E2 - G Tuning
Fourth G–C

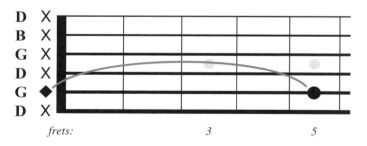

Fig. E3 - Standard Tuning
Fourth G–C

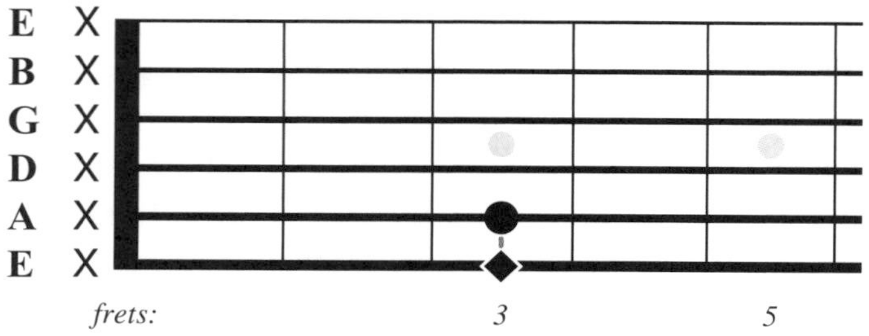

Fig. E4 - G Tuning
Fourth G–C

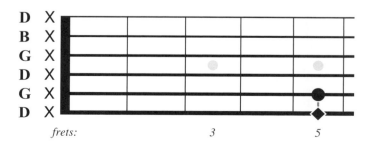

Keith Richards' G-Tuning Move

Intervallic shapes can be recognized on adjacent and nonadjacent strings. It's beneficial to learn all interval shapes in standard tuning and then see how they compare in whatever alternate tuning you're using. Certain tunings allow you to easily finger things that would be difficult or impossible in standard tuning. Take, for example, Keith Richards' signature move in G tuning (**Figs. F1** and **F2**):

Fig. F1 - G Tuning
C chord

Fig. F2 - G Tuning
Fadd9/C

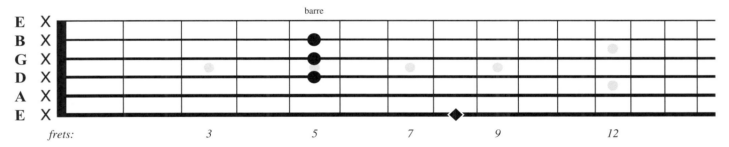

This is a finger twister in standard tuning yet easy as pie in G tuning. You can simulate this move in standard tuning (**Figs. F3** and **F4**) but it leaves out all the important G notes on top. It can be accessed in standard tuning, but not easily **(Fig. F5)**.

Fig. F3 - Standard Tuning C

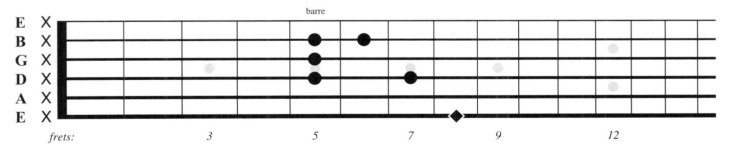

Fig. F4 - Standard Tuning F/C

Fig. F5 - Standard Tuning Fadd9/C

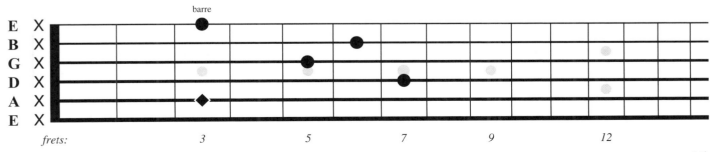

Chapter 3:
ANALYZING TUNINGS

I like to analyze a tuning as I get familiar with it. Where are the thirds? Where are the sixths, roots, and octaves? What is easier to play in the alternate tuning? What is more difficult? Messing around and discovering the key shapes that work easily and melodically in each tuning is an important part of the process. As you categorize intervallic shapes and relationships, notice the similarities and differences in comparison to other tunings. It's absolute magic to discover the happy accidents that occur when a familiar shape from one tuning is transplanted to another tuning.

Sometimes it works in an altogether different fashion. Each tuning is a mystery that unfolds in layers from string to string. I find it creatively refreshing and stimulating to discover the new melodic combinations that exist in every tuning. Try a 12-string in C tuning and watch as the intervallic relationships unfold **(Figs. G1–G2)**.

Fig. G1 - C Tuning Thirds in C Major

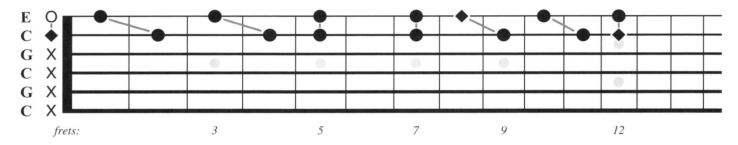

Fig. G2 - C Tuning Sixths in C Major

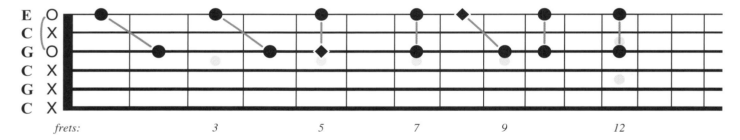

Notice that the sixth intervals in Fig. G2 are the same as in standard tuning **(Fig. G3)**. Since the strings are still tuned to G and E, they are good reference points.

Fig. G3 - Standard Tuning Sixths in C Major

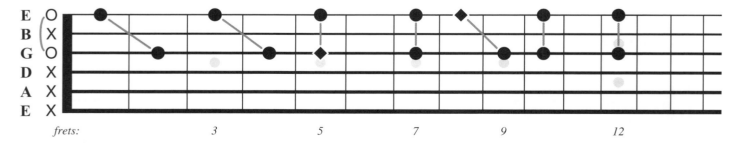

Here are the sixths in C tuning on the lower pairs of strings: fourth-and-third **(Fig. G4)** and sixth-and-fifth **(Fig. G5)**.

Fig. G4 - C Tuning Sixths in C Major

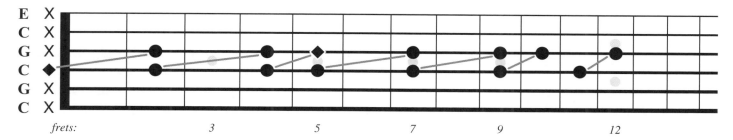

Fig. G5 - C Tuning Sixths in C Major

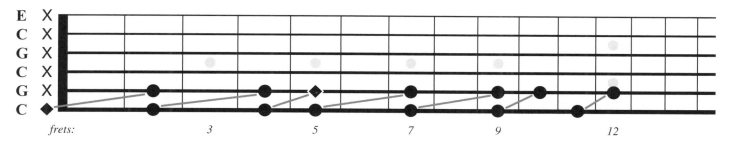

These sixth shapes in C tuning are recognizable to mandolin players, as the C to G relationship is a fifth and mandolins are tuned in fifths. It requires wide finger stretches to play these sixths on adjacent strings in standard tuning **(Fig. H1)**.

Fig. H1 - Standard Tuning Sixths in C Major

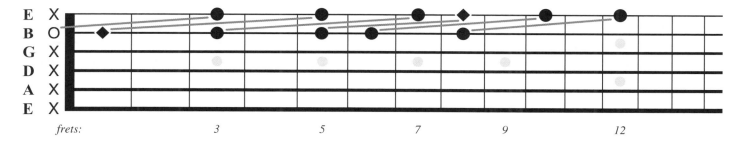

C tuning provides much smoother and more graceful sixth voicings **(Fig. H2)**.

Fig. H2 - C Tuning Sixths in C Major

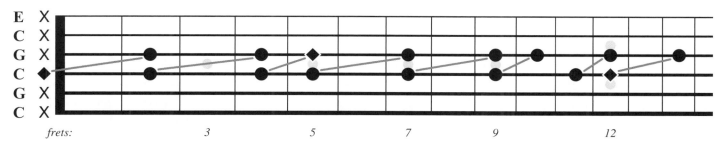

Tunings with Duplicate Pitches

Remember that when you have strings tuned to duplicate pitches (such as the C and G strings in C tuning) the shapes will duplicate themselves across the fretboard **(Fig. I)**.

Fig. I - C Tuning C Major

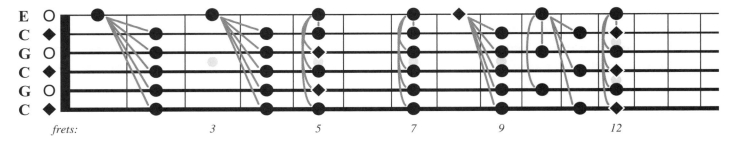

> The critical thing to recognize in this diagram is the relationship of the root (C) and fifth (G) degree strings to the only third (E) degree string, the high E. This is where the thirds, sixths, tenths, and thirteenths (the extended octave equivalents) exist.

This is useful in intervallic categorizing. In other words, these things sound good! They resonate glowingly across the neck and make many harmonious vibrations. This is only one aspect of the C-tuning, C-major web connection. You can see different relationships from string to string if you look for different ways to find the same or other intervals—sixths, for example **(Fig. J)**:

Fig. J - C Tuning Sixths in C Major

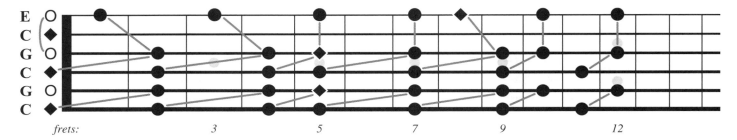

Endless Possibilities

There are thousands of possibilities. Remember, change one note of a tuning and the whole pattern shifts, but it shifts accordingly and reasonably as soon as you access the new shapes. Raise the high E string to F, for example (in C tuning C–G–C–G–C–F), and you get a suspended tuning similar to D–A–D–G–A–D **(Fig. K)**:

Fig. K - C Suspended Tuning C Major

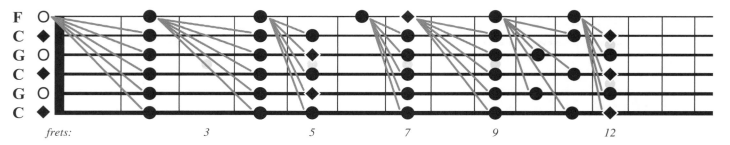

The spiderweb has shifted and new tonalities and shapes present themselves, but they're still organizable and useful. This tuning suggests different combinations, worse for some intervals and better for others. Remember, the only difference between it and C tuning is that the high E string has been raised to F **(Figs. K1–K2)**.

Fig. K1 - C Suspended Tuning C Major

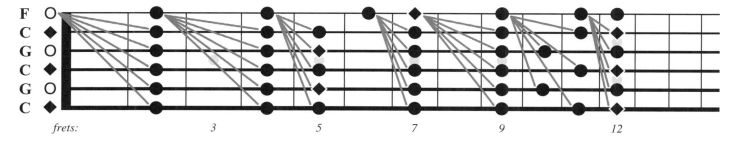

Fig. K2 - C Tuning C Major

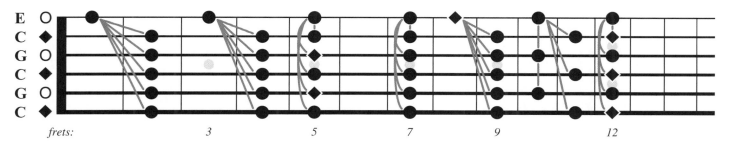

Categorizing Tunings by Interval

A good way to organize tunings is to categorize the intervals between the strings in each tuning.

Standard tuning is E–A–D–G–B–E, which can be represented in this form:				
E–A	A–D	D–G	G–B	B–E
fourth	fourth	fourth	major third	fourth
G tuning is D–G–D–G–B–D:				
D–G	G–D	D–G	G–B	B–D
fourth	fifth	fourth	major third	minor third
E tuning is E–B–E–G♯–B–E:				
E–B	B–E	E–G♯	G♯–B	B–E
fifth	fourth	major third	minor third	fourth
C tuning is C–G–C–G–C–E:				
C–G	G–C	C–G	G–C	C–E
fifth	fourth	fifth	fourth	major third
D–A–D–G–A–D:				
D–A	A–D	D–G	G–A	A–D
fifth	fourth	fourth	second	fourth

Keep these intervals in mind for each tuning and it will help you negotiate string-to-string melodies and navigate multiple tunings.

Major Scale Modes and Chords

To get the most out of the diagrams in this book it helps to have a basic understanding of how the seven modes of the major scale work and which chords they go with.

Key of C

1. The C major (Ionian) scale (C–D–E–F–G–A–B–C) goes with the I: major 7 chord (Cmaj7).
2. The D Dorian mode (D–E–F–G–A–B–C–D) goes with the ii: minor 7 chord (Dm7).
3. The E Phrygian mode (E–F–G–A–B–C–D–E) goes with the iii: minor 7 chord (Em7).
4. The F Lydian mode (F–G–A–B–C–D–E–F) goes with the IV: major 7 chord (Fmaj7).
5. The G Mixolydian mode (G–A–B–C–D–E–F–G) goes with the V: dominant 7 chord (G7).
6. The A Aeolian mode (A–B–C–D–E–F–G–A) goes with the vi: minor 7 chord (Am7).
7. The B Locrian mode (B–C–D–E–F–G–A–B) goes with the vii: minor 7 flat 5 chord (Bm7♭5).

Key of G

1. G major (Ionian) scale (G–A–B–C–D–E–F♯–G): Gmaj7
2. A Dorian (A–B–C–D–E–F♯–G–A): Am7
3. B Phrygian (B–C–D–E–F♯–G–A–B): Bm7
4. C Lydian (C–D–E–F♯–G–A–B–C): Cmaj7
5. D Mixolydian (D–E–F♯–G–A–B–C–D): D7
6. E Aeolian (E–F♯–G–A–B–C–D–E): Em7
7. F♯ Locrian (F♯–G–A–B–C–D–E–F♯): F♯m7♭5

Key of E

1. E major (Ionian) scale (E–F♯–G♯–A–B–C♯–D♯–E): Emaj7
2. F♯ Dorian (F♯–G♯–A–B–C♯–D♯–E–F♯): F♯m7
3. G♯ Phrygian (G♯–A–B–C♯–D♯–E–F♯–G♯): G♯m7
4. A Lydian (A–B–C♯–D♯–E–F♯–G♯–A): Amaj7
5. B Mixolydian (B–C♯–D♯–E–F♯–G♯–A–B): B7
6. C♯ Aeolian (C♯–D♯–E–F♯–G♯–A–B–C♯): C♯m7
7. D♯ Locrian (D♯–E–F♯–G♯–A–B–C♯–D♯): D♯m7♭5

It is the chord progression and key that determines the proper use of a particular mode. For example, Cmaj7 in C is the I chord, therefore you would use a C major scale to play over it. C major 7 in G is the IV chord, therefore you would use a C Lydian scale to play over it. Also bear in mind the subtle differences in scales. The difference between the Dorian and Aeolian modes, for instance, is the sixth tone.

C Dorian

C	D	E♭	F	G	A	B♭	C
1	2	♭3	4	5	6	♭7	1

C Aeolian

C	D	E♭	F	G	A♭	B♭	C
1	2	♭3	4	5	♭6	♭7	1

C Dorian is useful when playing over Cm7–F7, a chord progression that has an A note. C Aeolian would be useful in playing over Cm7–A♭, a chord progression that has an A♭ note.

C Dorian is derived from the B♭ major scale:

B♭	C	D	E♭	F	G	A	B♭
1	2	3	4	5	6	7	1

It is the second mode: C–D–E♭–F–G–A–B♭–C.

C Aeolian is derived from the E♭ major scale:

E♭	F	G	A♭	B♭	C	D	E♭
1	2	3	4	5	6	7	1

It is the sixth mode: C–D–E♭–F–G–A♭–B♭–C.

A working knowledge of keys and modes is helpful in using the information in the fretboard maps on the following pages. However, even if you approach the diagrams from a totally fresh and uninformed point of view, there's plenty of information here to inspire every player. Each diagram represents a tonality to improvise in. The more you know about how music fits together the easier it will be to switch quickly from one color to another while playing. I often sit in front of a tuning map and find new possibilities of fingering combinations, and I am very familiar with these tunings, having used them for many years. The thrill of discovery is constant and never ending when putting tones together—the variations are inspirational. Each tuning presents musical and mathematically unique formations. Exploration of tonalities remains the goal.

Chapter 4:

STANDARD TUNING FRETBOARD MAPS

Comparing Scales

The following diagrams highlight the variable tones in comparative scales. The C major scale is C–D–E–F–G–A–B–C. C Mixolydian is C–D–E–F–G–A–B♭–C. Notice that the only difference is the seventh tone, which is flatted in the Mixolydian mode.

C major: C–D–E–F–G–A–B–C

C Mixolydian: C–D–E–F–G–A–B♭–C

C Major - Standard Tuning

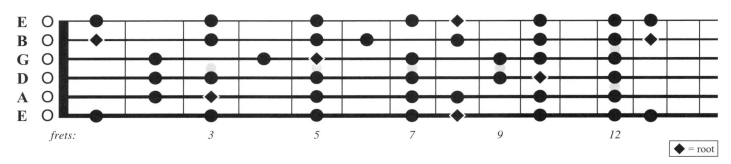

♦ = root

C Mixolydian - Standard Tuning   F Major, 5th mode

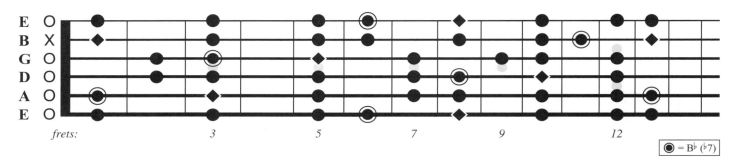

◉ = B♭ (♭7)

C Dorian is C–D–E♭–F–G–A–B♭–C. Notice that the only difference between this and C Mixolydian is the third tone, which is flatted in the Dorian mode.

C Mixolydian: C–D–E–F–G–A–B♭–C

C Dorian: C–D–E♭–F–G–A–B♭–C

C Dorian - Standard Tuning   B♭ Major, 2nd mode

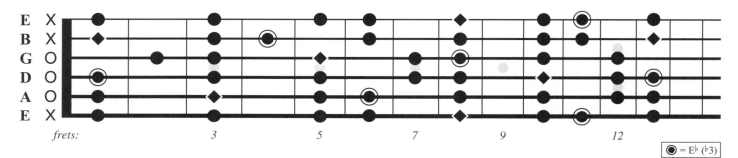

◉ = E♭ (♭3)

C major pentatonic is C–D–E–G–A–C, the root, second, third, fifth, and sixth of the C major scale.

C major: C–D–E–F–G–A–B–C

C major pentatonic: C–D–E–G–A–C

C Major Pentatonic

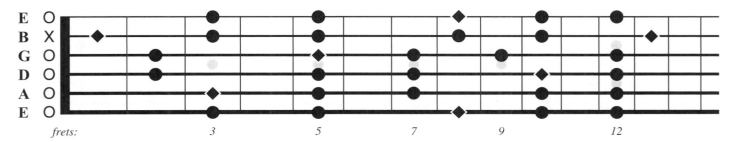

C minor pentatonic is C–E♭–F–G–B♭–C, the root, third, fourth, fifth, and seventh of the C Dorian scale.

C Dorian: C–D–E♭–F–G–A–B♭–C

C minor pentatonic: C–E♭–F–G–B♭–C

C Minor Pentatonic

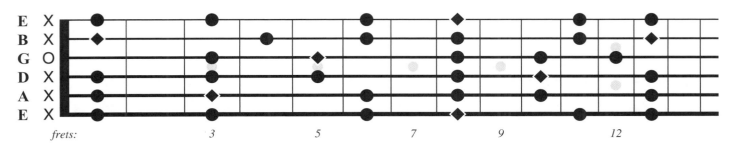

The C Aeolian mode is C–D–E♭–F–G–A♭–B♭–C. Notice that the only difference between this and C Dorian (C–D–E♭–F–G–A–B♭–C), is the sixth, which is flatted in the Aeolian mode.

C Dorian: C–D–E♭–F–G–A–B♭–C

C Aeolian: C–D–E♭–F–G–A♭–B♭–C

C Dorian - Standard Tuning B♭ Major, 2nd mode

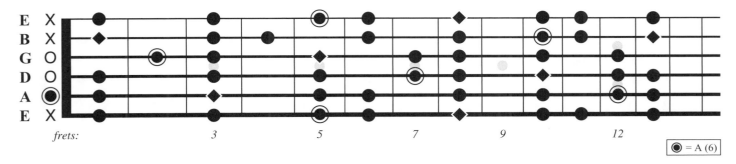

◉ = A (6)

C Aeolian - Standard Tuning E♭ Major, 6th mode

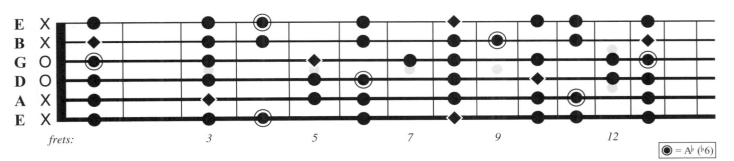

◉ = A♭ (♭6)

23

The C Phrygian mode is C–D♭–E♭–F–G–A♭–B♭–C. Notice that the only difference between this and the C Aeolian mode is the second tone, which is flatted in the Phrygian mode.

C Aeolian: C–D–E♭–F–G–A♭–B♭–C

C Phrygian: C–D♭–E♭–F–G–A♭–B♭–C

C Phrygian - Standard Tuning   A♭ Major, 3rd mode

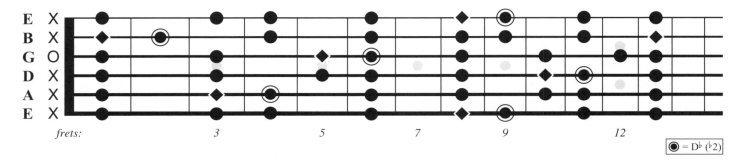

The fifth mode of the F harmonic minor scale is C–D♭–E–F–G–A♭–B♭–C. The only difference between this and C Phrygian is the third tone, which is raised to E for the F harmonic minor (fifth mode).

C Phrygian: C–D♭–E♭–F–G–A♭–B♭–C

F harmonic minor (fifth mode): C–D♭–E–F–G–A♭–B♭–C

Fifth Mode of F Harmonic Minor - Standard Tuning

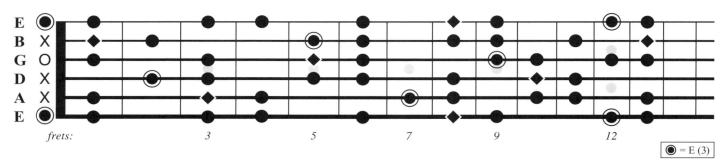

F Harmonic Minor (F–G–A♭–B♭–C–D♭–E–F) - Standard Tuning

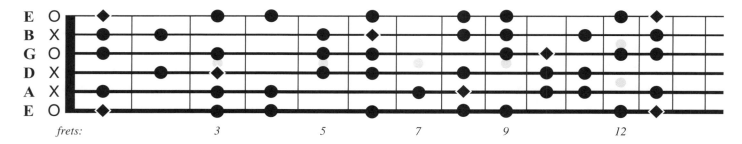

Chapter 5:
G TUNING AND THE SPIDERWEB

G Tuning: D–G–D–G–B–D

This chapter introduces the concept I call the "spiderweb." The connecting lines illustrate combinations that use the B string to represent thirds and sixths and their extended tenths and thirteenths. I advise you to experiment with the paired strings, connected with lines, to discover the melodic scale intervals that occur within each tuning and each step of the scale. Try droning open strings while playing connected intervals up and down the neck in scales of thirds, sixths, tenths, and thirteenths, paying special attention to the shapes and the way they shift in G tuning.

I call the B string the pivot string. It represents the third of the major scale and is the key to connecting the root (G) and the fifth (D) degree strings. It is the central point of gravity that pulls the various intervals together and creates the magic tonal shapes. Pay special attention to the intervals that are created in combination with the B string as it is the only nonduplicated chord tone.

It is also helpful to realize that these spiderweb shapes repeat themselves, in exactly the same way, on the fretboard starting at various points according to the major scale they represent. For example, starting on the fifth fret for C major as compared to G major, the shapes shift accordingly from frets 0–12 in G major to frets 5–17 for C major. This is where a capo comes in handy. To play comfortably in the key of C major (in G tuning, using open strings) capo at the fifth fret.

Keith Richards is probably the most well-known master of G tuning. Robert Johnson, Bonnie Raitt, Lowell George, and Jackson Browne frequently tuned G tuning up a whole step to A tuning (E–A–E–A–C#–E) and created endless amounts of beauty using the same shapes as G tuning, yet resonating a whole step higher. Put on anything by these artists and be happy you have ears and fingers!

G Major (G–A–B–C–D–E–F#–G) - G Tuning

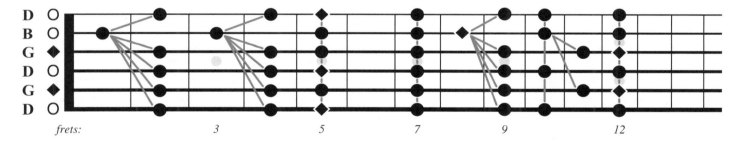

G Mixolydian (G–A–B–C–D–E–F–G) - G Tuning C Major, 5th mode

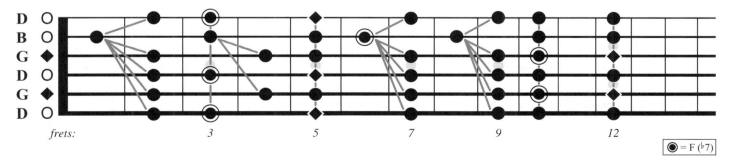

◉ = F (♭7)

G Dorian (G–A–B♭–C–D–E–F–G) - G Tuning   F Major, 2nd mode

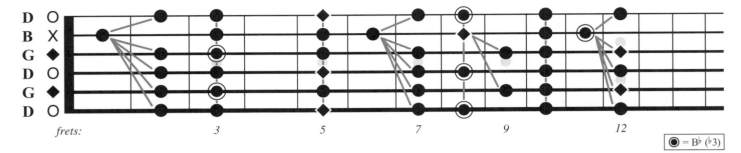

G Major Pentatonic (G–A–B–D–E–G) - G Tuning

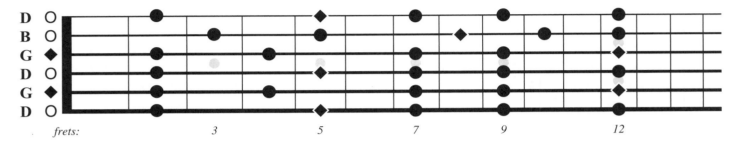

G Minor Pentatonic (G–B♭–C–D–F–G) - G Tuning   B♭ Major Pentatonic, 5th mode

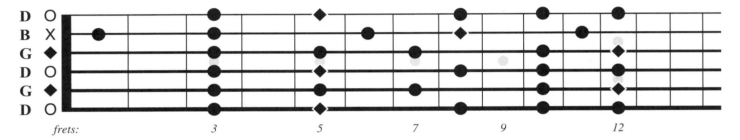

G Dorian (G–A–B♭–C–D–E–F–G) - G Tuning   F Major, 2nd mode

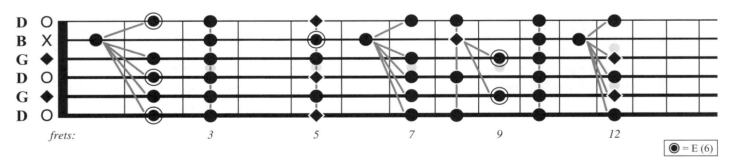

G Aeolian (G–A–B♭–C–D–E♭–F–G) - G Tuning   B♭ Major, 6th mode

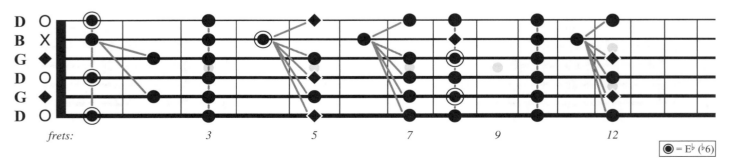

G Phrygian (G–A♭–B♭–C–D–E♭–F–G) - G Tuning E♭ Major, 3rd mode

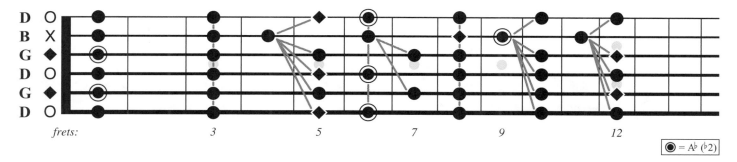

Fifth Mode of C Harmonic Minor (G–A♭–B–C–D–E♭–F–G) - G Tuning

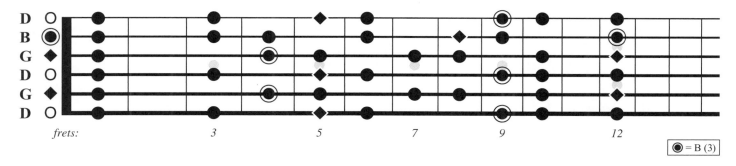

C Harmonic Minor (C–D–E♭–F–G–A♭–B–C) - G Tuning

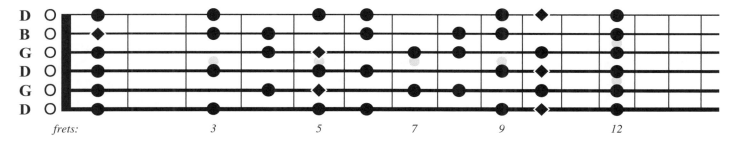

G-Tuning Examples

G Major Intervals

Open G Tuning:
① = D   ④ = D
② = B   ⑤ = G
③ = G   ⑥ = D

Track 1

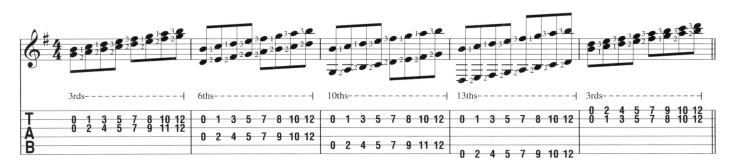

27

G Mixolydian Intervals

Track 2

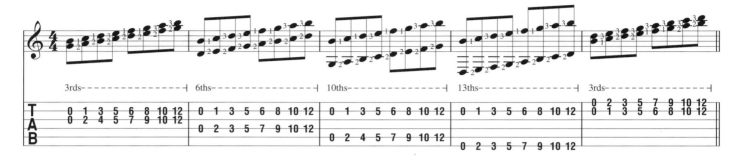

G Minor Pentatonic Scale

Track 3

G Major Pentatonic Scale

Track 4

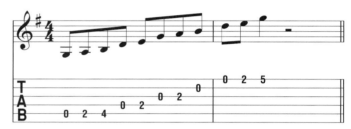

G Slide Lick #1

Track 5

G Slide Lick #2

Track 6

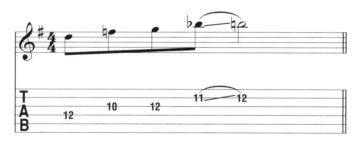

G Slide Lick #3

Track 7

G Slide Lick #4

Track 8

G-Tuning Songs

Slack-Key Tuned Down a Whole Step - *G Major*

Open G Tuning,
Tune Down 1 Step:
① = C ④ = C
② = A ⑤ = F
③ = F ⑥ = C

Electric Slide - *G Major*

Track 10

Open G Tuning:
①= D ④= D
②= B ⑤= G
③= G ⑥= D

Freely ♩ = 100

w/ slide, delay & vol. pedal

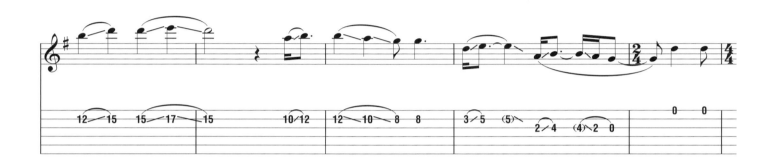

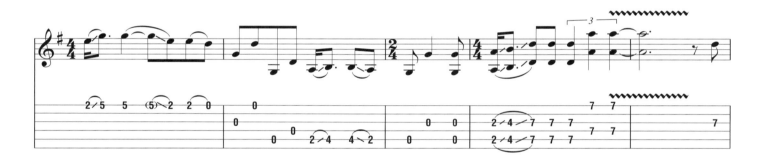

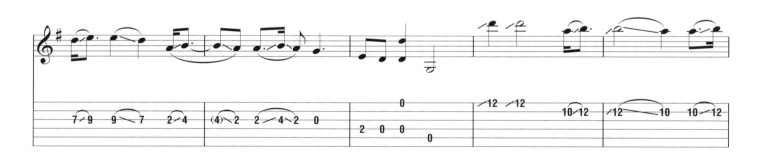

Blues Shuffle - *G Minor Pentatonic*

Open G Tuning:
①= D ④= D
②= B ⑤= G
③= G ⑥= D

♩ = 68

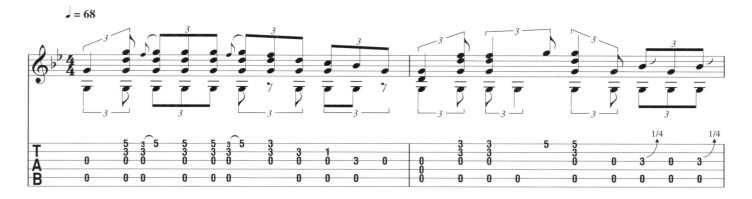

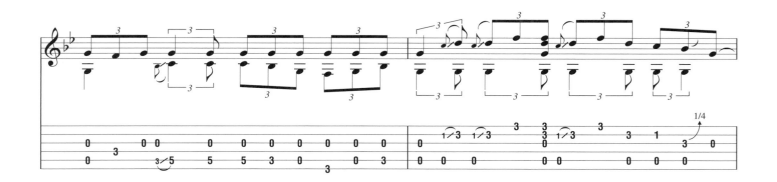

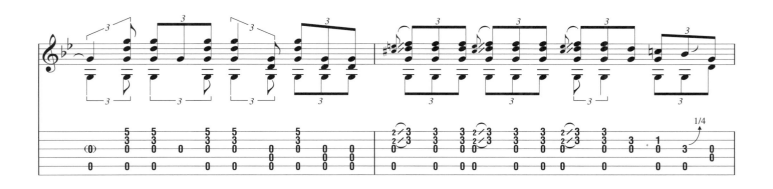

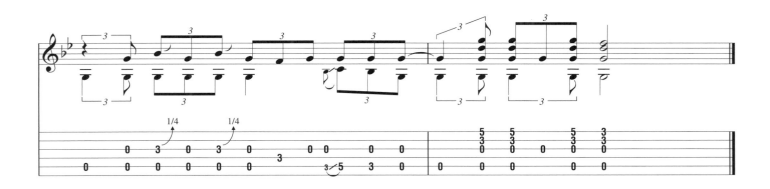

31

Acoustic Slide - *G Minor Pentatonic*

Open G Tuning:
① = D ④ = D
② = B ⑤ = G
③ = G ⑥ = D

Track 12

♩ = 95

w/ slide

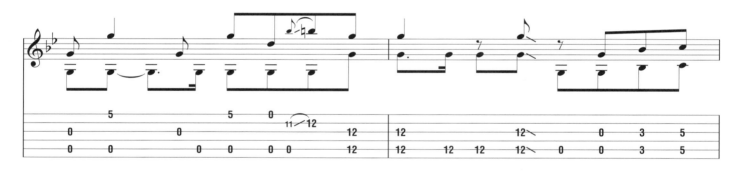

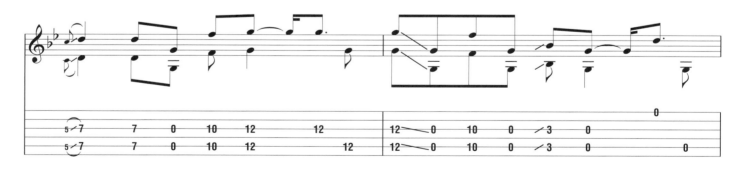

rit.

32

C Harmonic Minor, Fifth Mode

Open G Tuning:
① = D ④ = D
② = B ⑤ = G
③ = G ⑥ = D

Track 13

Freely ♩ = 74

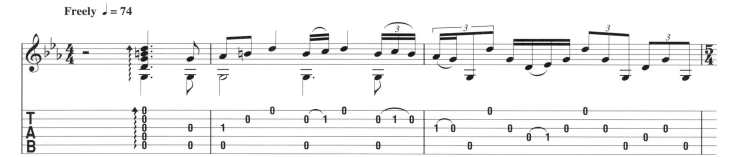

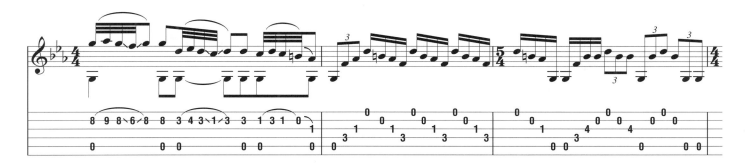

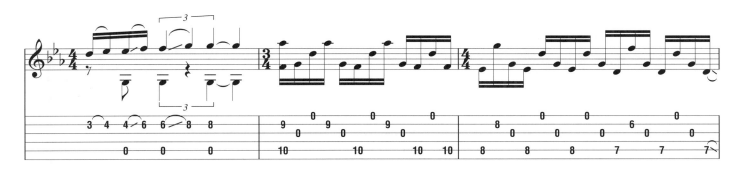

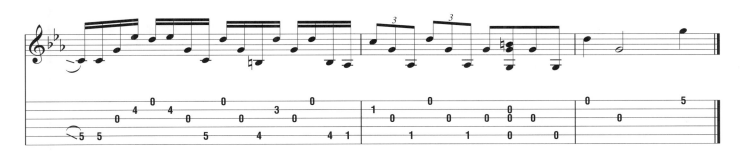

D Mixolydian Sitar Cross Guitar

Open G Tuning:
① = D ④ = D
② = B ⑤ = G
③ = G ⑥ = D

Freely ♩ = 70

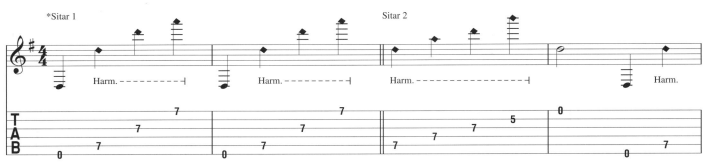

*Sitar 1

Sitar 2

*Sitar 1 continues 2-bar drone pattern throughout.

♩ = 132

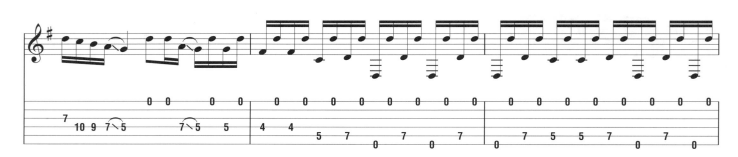

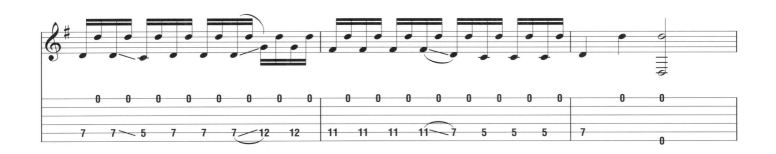

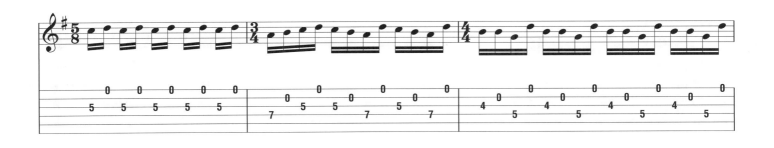

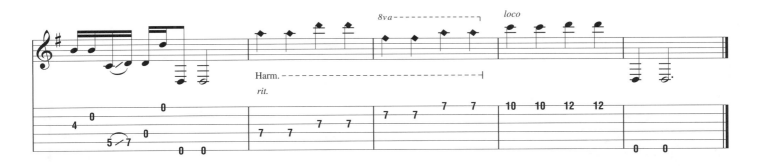

35

Chapter 6:

E TUNING

In E tuning (E-B-E-G♯-B-E) the G string (retuned to G♯) becomes the pivot string. All the spiderweb lines lead from this string. The G♯ tone is the third of the E chord, just as the B string is the third in G tuning. The shapes have shifted, yet they remain similar in design. Throw down some Elmore James, Jesse Ed Davis, Duane Allman, David Lindley, or Ry Cooder to experience the possibilities, although they frequently tuned E tuning down a whole step to D (D-A-D-F♯-A-D). All the shapes in E and D tuning are the same, they simply resonate a whole step lower in E tuning.

Notice also that the root in E tuning is on the low sixth string (as compared to the fifth string in G tuning). This should be kept in mind while creating root drones. Also notice that the fifth has shifted from the sixth string in G tuning to the fifth string in E tuning.

Footnote on David Lindley: You could give him one string tuned to a random pitch, make him play it with his teeth, and it would still sound great!

E Major (E-F♯-G♯-A-B-C♯-D♯-E) - E Tuning

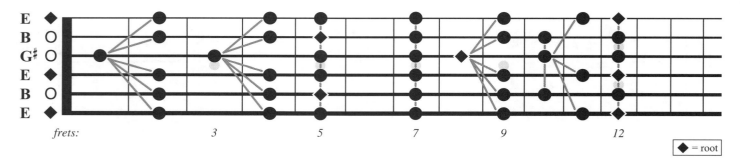

E Mixolydian (E-F♯-G♯-A-B-C♯-D-E) - E Tuning A Major, 5th mode

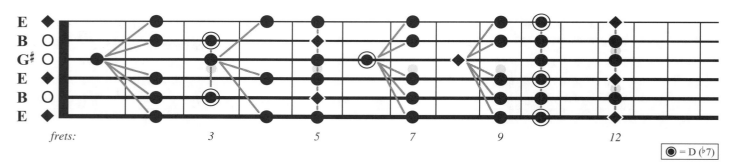

E Dorian (E-F♯-G-A-B-C♯-D-E) - E Tuning D Major, 2nd mode

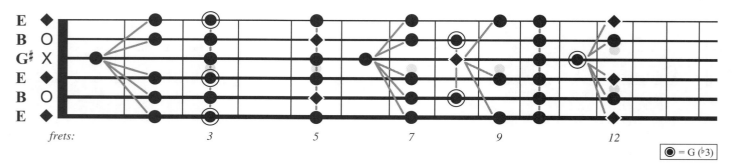

E Major Pentatonic (E–F♯–G♯–B–C♯–E) – E Tuning

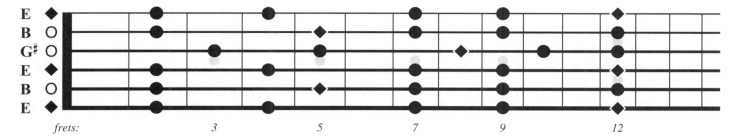

E Minor Pentatonic (E–G–A–B–D–E) – E Tuning G Major Pentatonic, 5th mode

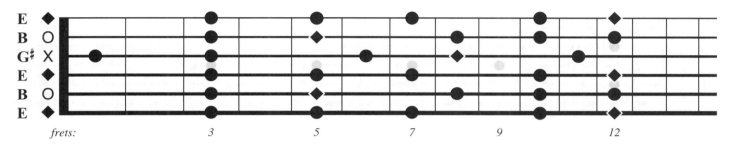

E Dorian (E–F♯–G–A–B–C♯–D–E) – E Tuning D Major, 2nd mode

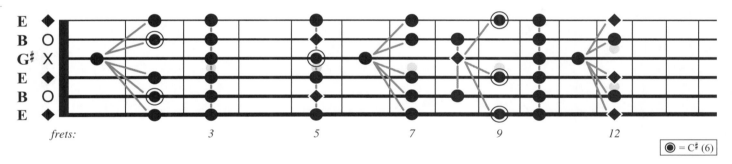

⬤ = C♯ (6)

E Aeolian (E–F♯–G–A–B–C–D–E) – E Tuning G Major, 6th mode

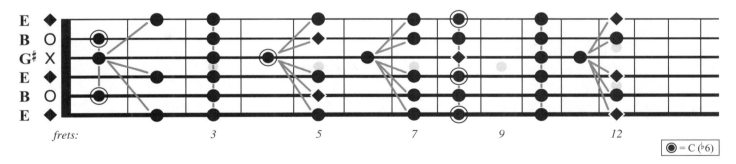

⬤ = C (♭6)

E Phrygian (E–F–G–A–B–C–D–E) – E Tuning C Major, 3rd mode

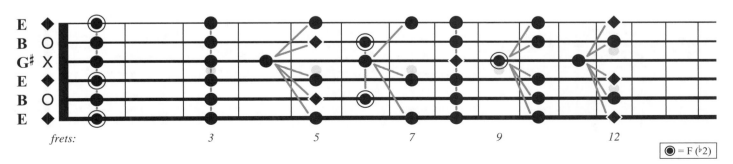

⬤ = F (♭2)

Fifth Mode of A Harmonic Minor (E–F–G#–A–B–C–D–E) – E Tuning

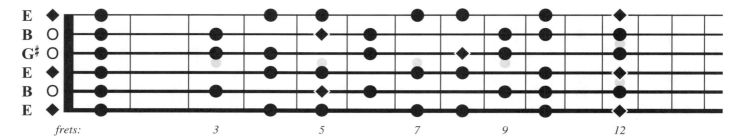

A Harmonic Minor (A–B–C–D–E–F–G#–A) – E Tuning

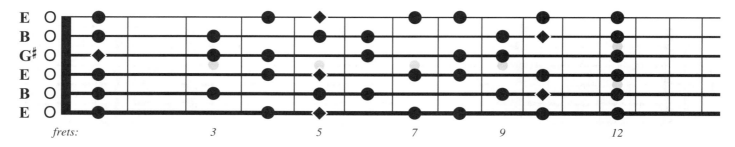

E-Tuning Examples

E Major Intervals

Open E Tuning:
①= E ④= E
②= B ⑤= B
③= G# ⑥= E

Track 15

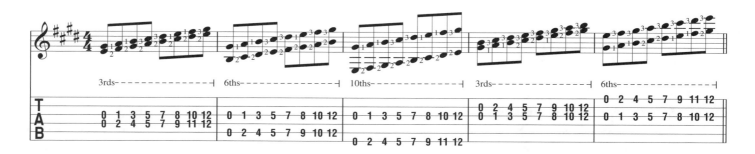

E Mixolydian Intervals

Open E Tuning:
①= E ④= E
②= B ⑤= B
③= G# ⑥= E

Track 16

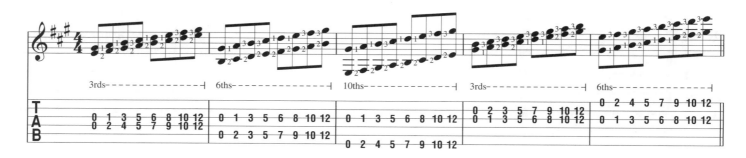

E Minor Pentatonic Scale

Open E Tuning:
①= E ④= E
②= B ⑤= B
③= G# ⑥= E

Track 17

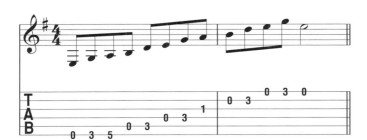

E Major Pentatonic Scale

Open E Tuning:
①= E ④= E
②= B ⑤= B
③= G# ⑥= E

Track 18

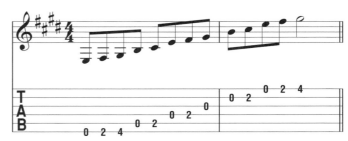

E Slide Lick #1

Open E Tuning:
①= E ④= E
②= B ⑤= B
③= G# ⑥= E

Track 19

E Slide Lick #2

Open E Tuning:
①= E ④= E
②= B ⑤= B
③= G# ⑥= E

Track 20

E Slide Lick #3

Open E Tuning:
①= E ④= E
②= B ⑤= B
③= G# ⑥= E

Track 21

E Slide Lick #4

Open E Tuning:
①= E ④= E
②= B ⑤= B
③= G# ⑥= E

Track 22

E-Tuning Song

E Minor Pentatonic Slide

Open E Tuning:
① = E ④ = E
② = B ⑤ = B
③ = G# ⑥ = E

Track 23

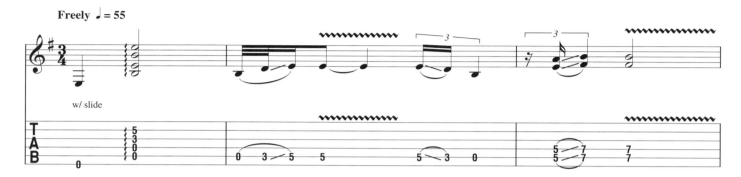

Chapter 7

C TUNING

In C tuning (C–G–C–G–C–E), the pivot string (the third of the chord) has shifted yet again. Now the first string is tuned to the third of the C chord (E) and all the spiderweb lines emanate from it. This creates a new, yet similar, symmetry. Notice that the root is on the sixth string (tuned down to C) and the fifth is on the fifth string (tuned down to G). To blow and expand your mind completely, listen to Leo Kottke.

C Major (C–D–E–F–G–A–B–C) - C Tuning

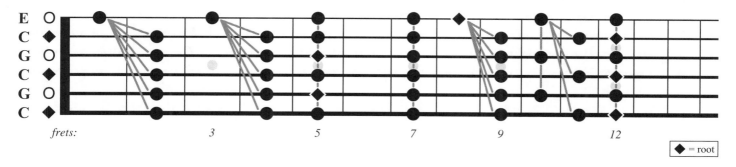

C Mixolydian (C–D–E–F–G–A–B♭–C) - C Tuning F Major, 5th mode

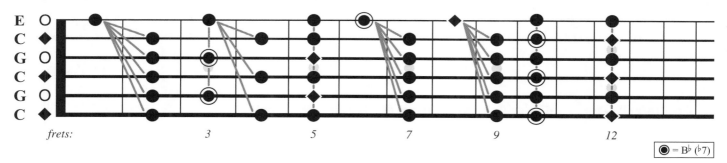

C Dorian (C–D–E♭–F–G–A–B♭–C) - C Tuning B♭ Major, 2nd mode

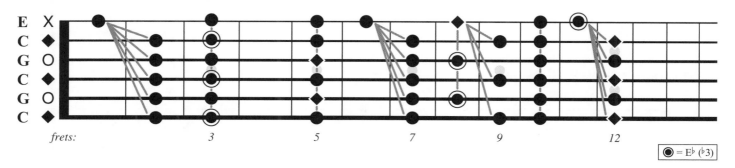

41

C Major Pentatonic (C–D–E–G–A–C) - C Tuning

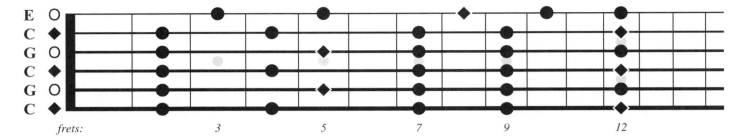

C Minor Pentatonic (C–E♭–F–G–B♭–C) - C Tuning   E♭ Major Pentatonic, 5th mode

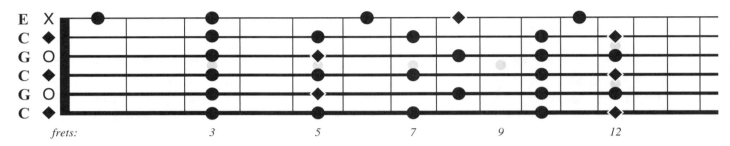

C Dorian (C–D–E♭–F–G–A–B♭–C) - C Tuning   B♭ Major, 2nd mode

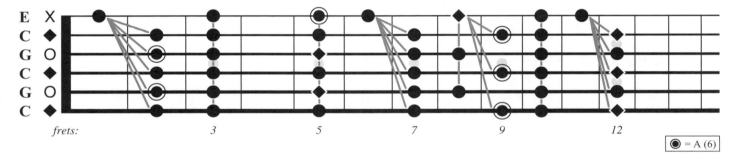

◉ = A (6)

C Aeolian (C–D–E♭–F–G–A♭–B♭–C) - C Tuning   E♭ Major, 6th mode

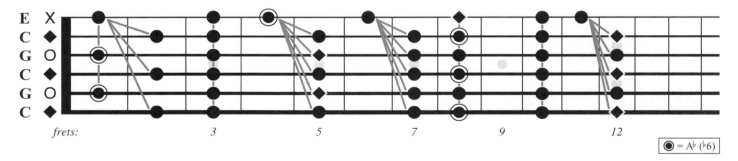

◉ = A♭ (♭6)

C Phrygian (C–D♭–E♭–F–G–A♭–B♭–C) - C Tuning   A♭ Major, 3rd mode

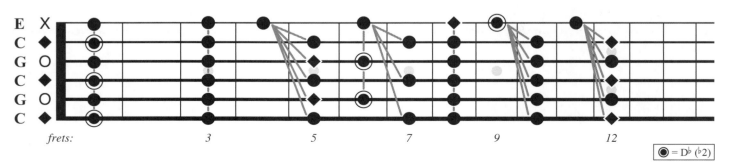

◉ = D♭ (♭2)

42

Fifth Mode of F Harmonic Minor (C–D♭–E–F–G–A♭–B♭–C) – C Tuning

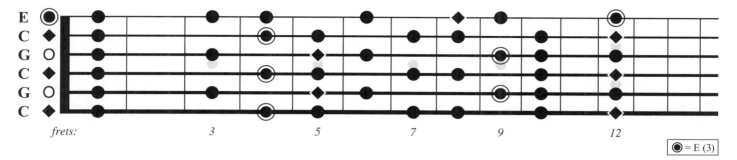

F Harmonic Minor (F–G–A♭–B♭–C–D♭–E–F)

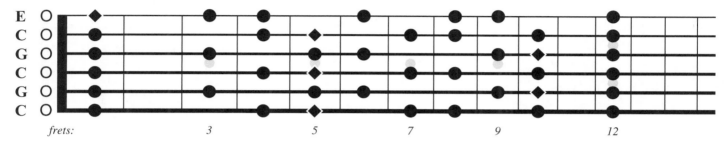

C-Tuning Examples

C Major Intervals

Open C Tuning:
① = E ④ = C
② = C ⑤ = G
③ = G ⑥ = C

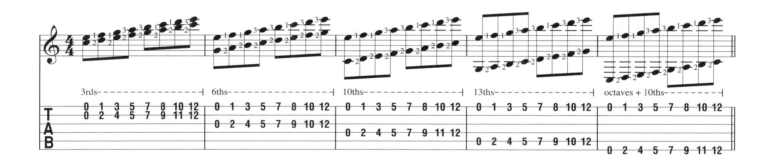

C Mixolydian Intervals

Open C Tuning:
① = E ④ = C
② = C ⑤ = G
③ = G ⑥ = C

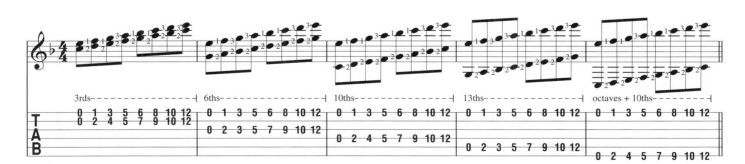

43

C Minor Pentatonic Scale

Open C Tuning:
①= E ④= C
②= C ⑤= G
③= G ⑥= C

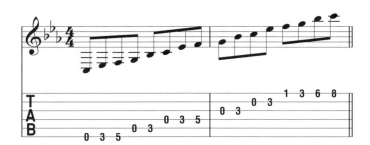

C Major Pentatonic Scale

Open C Tuning:
①= E ④= C
②= C ⑤= G
③= G ⑥= C

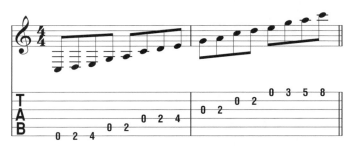

C Slide Lick #1

Open C Tuning:
①= E ④= C
②= C ⑤= G
③= G ⑥= C

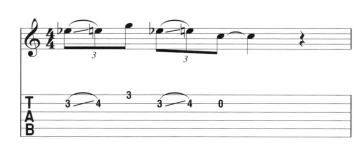

C Slide Lick #2

Open C Tuning:
①= E ④= C
②= C ⑤= G
③= G ⑥= C

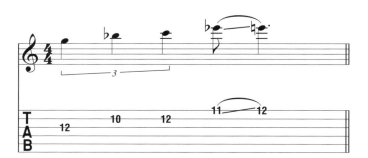

C Slide Lick #3

Open C Tuning:
①= E ④= C
②= C ⑤= G
③= G ⑥= C

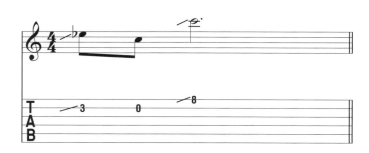

C Slide Lick #4

Open C Tuning:
①= E ④= C
②= C ⑤= G
③= G ⑥= C

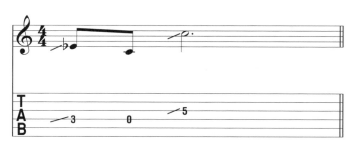

C-Tuning Songs

Fingerpicking with Slide

Open C Tuning:
①= E ④= C
②= C ⑤= G
③= G ⑥= C

Track 32

Freely ♩= 105

w/ slide

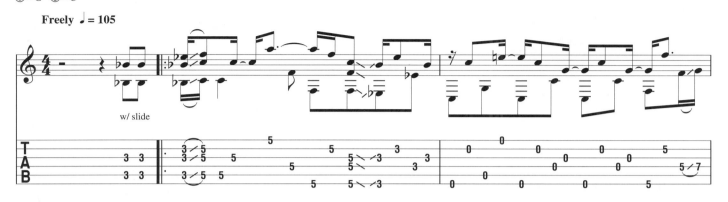

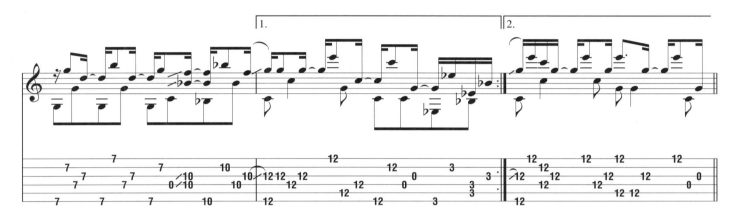

rit.

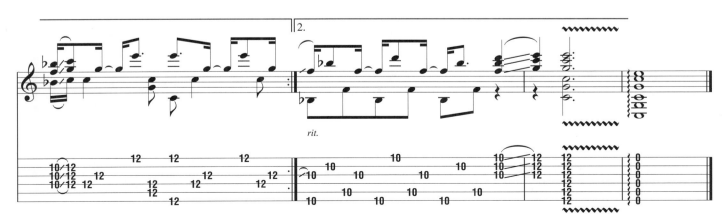

12-String Fingerpicking - *C Major*

Open C Tuning:
① = E ④ = C
② = C ⑤ = G
③ = G ⑥ = C

♩ = 104

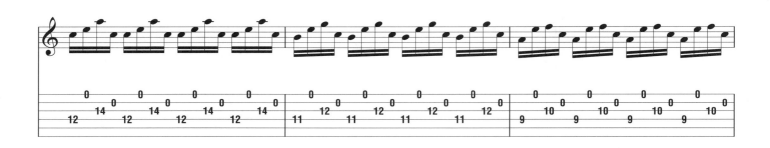

46

Chapter 8

D–A–D–G–A–D TUNING

D-A-D-G-A-D represents a departure from the open major-chord tunings, so there is no longer an easy web to follow. In D-A-D-G-A-D it is best to think in terms of dropped-D tuning on the bottom four strings (which is duplicated one step lower in C tuning, C-G-C-G-C-E). The only other thing to compensate for is the tuning of the top two strings, which have each been lowered a whole tone, so you must remember this while improvising. They still, however, are tuned to a fourth so the interval shapes will be just like standard tuning, except they are played two frets higher in D-A-D-G-A-D than in standard tuning. I think of D-A-D-G-A-D as dropped D on the bottom four strings and the key of E on the top two strings. Or you can just experiment and see what happens! Pierre Bensusan is the man to see about this one. D-A-D-G-A-D tuning lends itself very well to Celtic music.

D Major (D–E–F♯–G–A–B–C♯–D) - D–A–D–G–A–D Tuning

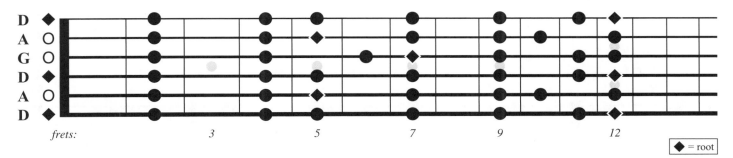

D Mixolydian (D–E–F♯–G–A–B–C–D) - D–A–D–G–A–D Tuning   G Major, 5th mode

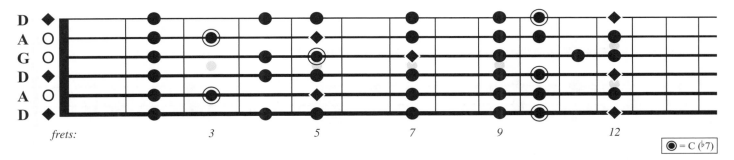

D Dorian (D–E–F–G–A–B–C–D) - D–A–D–G–A–D Tuning   C Major, 2nd mode

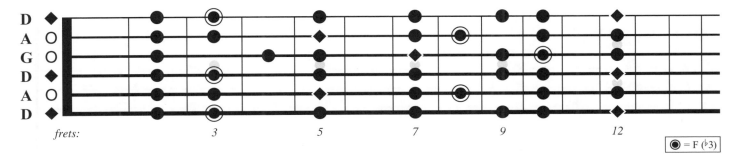

D Major Pentatonic (D-E-F#-A-B-D) - D-A-D-G-A-D Tuning

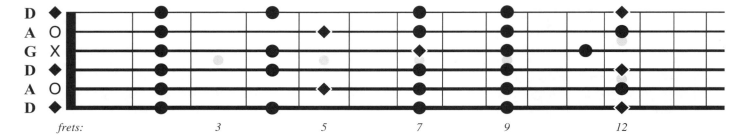

D Minor Pentatonic (D-F-G-A-C-D) - D-A-D-G-A-D Tuning

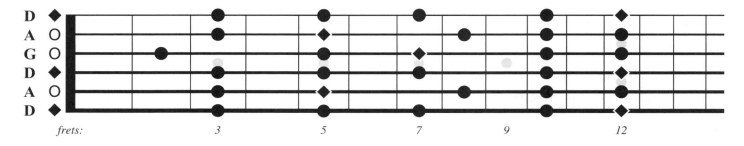

D Dorian (D-E-F-G-A-B-C-D) - D-A-D-G-A-D Tuning C Major, 2nd mode

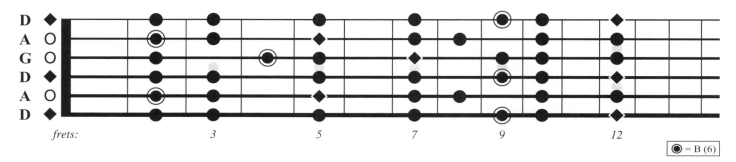

◉ = B (6)

D Aeolian (D-E-F-G-A-B♭-C-D) - D-A-D-G-A-D Tuning F Major, 6th mode

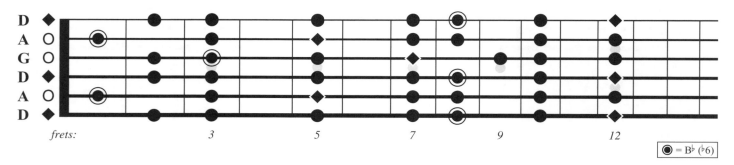

◉ = B♭ (♭6)

D Phrygian (D-E♭-F-G-A-B♭-C-D) - D-A-D-G-A-D Tuning B♭ Major, 3rd mode

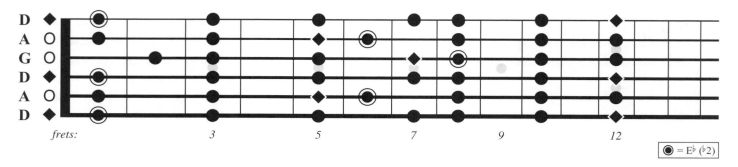

◉ = E♭ (♭2)

48

Fifth Mode of G Harmonic Minor (D–E♭–F♯–G–A–B♭–C–D) – D-A-D-G-A-D Tuning

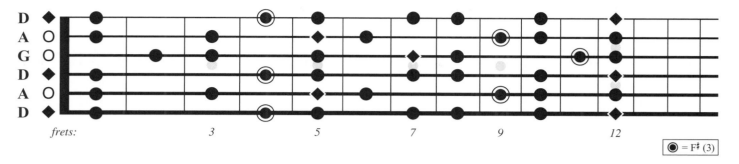

⦿ = F♯ (3)

G Harmonic Minor (G–A–B♭–C–D–E♭–F♯–G) – D-A-D-G-A-D Tuning

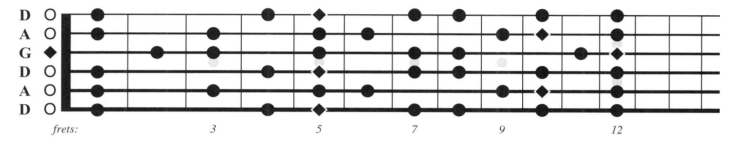

D-A-D-G-A-D Songs

Strumming in D-A-D-G-A-D - *D Major*

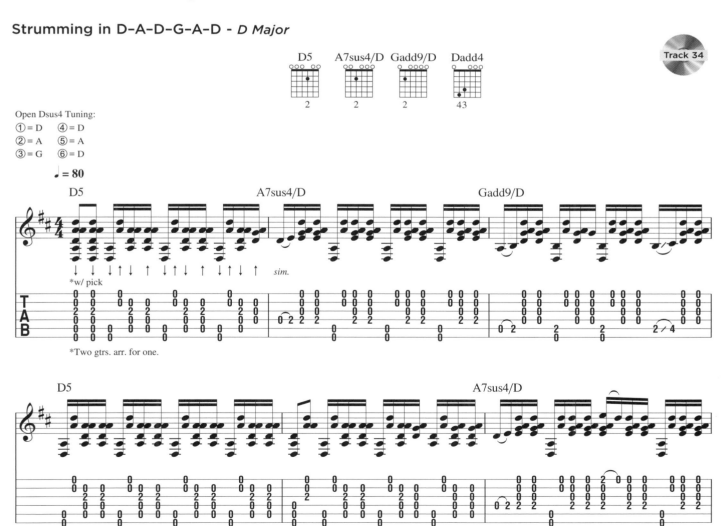

Track 34

49

Celtic Fingerpicking - *D Mixolydian*

Open Dsus4 Tuning:
① = D ④ = D
② = A ⑤ = A
③ = G ⑥ = D

fade out

Chapter 9:

MINOR TUNINGS

G Minor Tuning

There is only one difference between G minor (D–G–D–G–B♭–D) and G tuning (D–G–D–G–B–D): the B string has been lowered a half step to B♭. This lends itself to expressing minor tonalities with ease rather than dancing around the open B string in G tuning. Inspired by Sonny Landreth, I started fooling around with minor tunings and discovered that lots of possibilities exist in these realms.

I'll start by exploring the differences between G minor and G major tuning for the minor pentatonic and Dorian scales.

G Minor Pentatonic (G–B♭–C–D–F–G) - G Minor Tuning

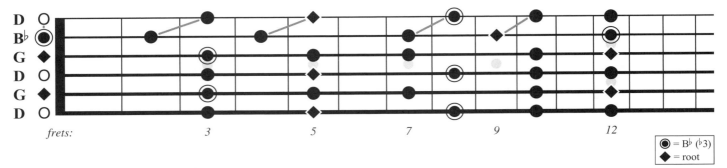

G Minor Pentatonic (G–B♭–C–D–F–G) - G Major Tuning

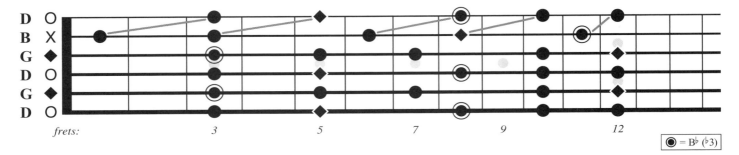

G Dorian (G–A–B♭–C–D–E–F–G) - G Minor Tuning

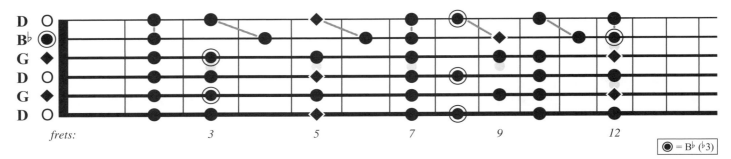

G Dorian (G–A–B♭–C–D–E–F–G) - G Major Tuning

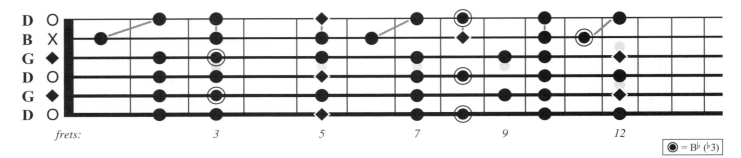

G Dorian (G-A-B♭-C-D-E-F-G) - G Minor Tuning F Major, 2nd mode

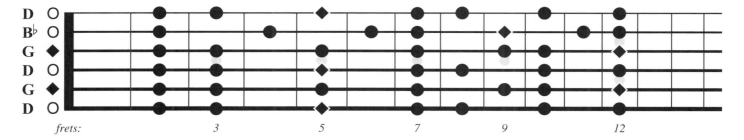

G Aeolian (G-A-B♭-C-D-E♭-F-G) - G Minor Tuning B♭ Major, 6th mode

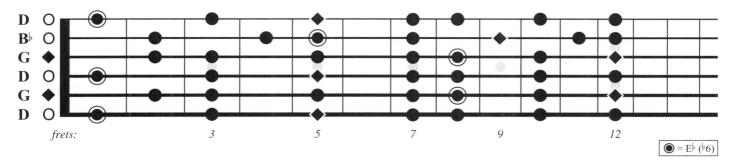

◉ = E♭ (♭6)

G Phrygian (G-A♭-B♭-C-D-E♭-F-G) - G Minor Tuning E♭ Major, 3rd mode

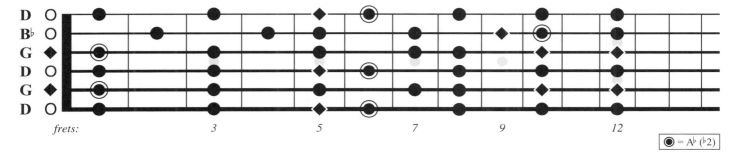

◉ = A♭ (♭2)

E Minor Tuning

The only difference between E minor (E-B-E-G-B-E) and E major tuning (E-B-E-G♯-B-E) is that the G string remains natural rather than tuned up one half step. This is an interesting situation because the top three strings (G, B, E) are tuned as they are in standard tuning, but the bottom three strings feel like dropped D tuned one step higher. So you can split the fretboard in half and play normally on the G, B, and E strings, while keeping bass lines going on the bottom three. For pure mastery of this tuning, check out Bukka White and Skip James. We'll start out by looking at the difference between E minor and E major tunings with the minor pentatonic and Dorian scales.

E Minor Pentatonic (E-G-A-B-D-E) - E Minor Tuning

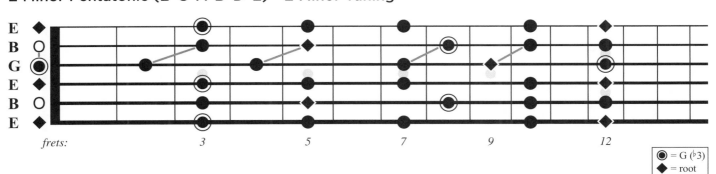

◉ = G (♭3)
◆ = root

53

E Minor Pentatonic (E-G-A-B-D-E) - E Major Tuning

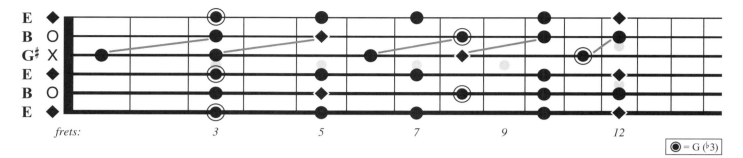

◉ = G (♭3)

E Dorian (E-F♯-G-A-B-C♯-D-E) - E Minor Tuning

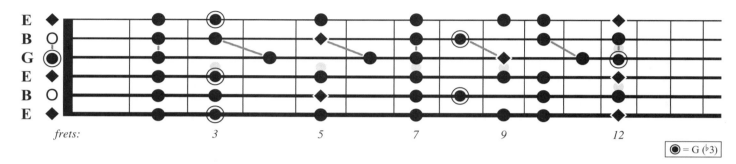

◉ = G (♭3)

E Dorian (E-F♯-G-A-B-C♯-D-E) - E Major Tuning

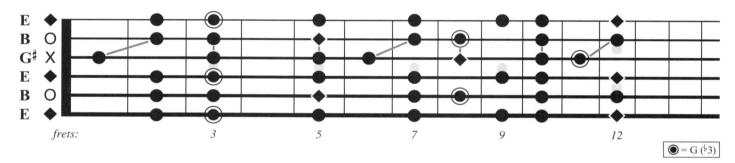

◉ = G (♭3)

E Dorian (E-F♯-G-A-B-C♯-D-E) - E Minor Tuning D Major, 2nd mode

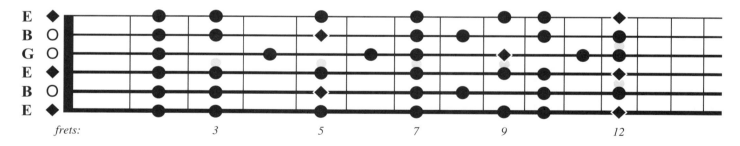

E Aeolian (E-F♯-G-A-B-C-D-E) - E Minor Tuning G Major, 6th mode

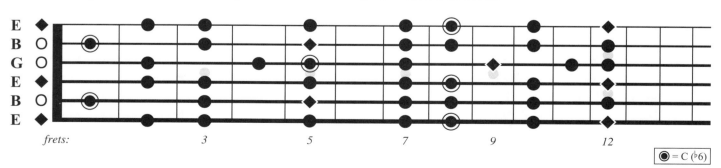

◉ = C (♭6)

54

E Phrygian (E-F-G-A-B-C-D-E) - E Minor Tuning C Major, 3rd mode

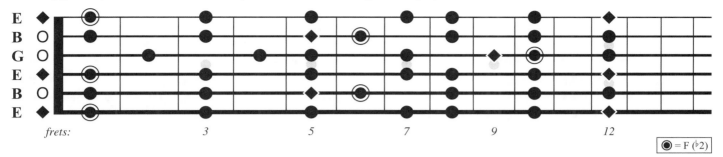

E
B
G
E
B
E

frets: 3 5 7 9 12

◉ = F (♭2)

C Minor Tuning

The difference between C minor tuning (C-G-C-G-C-E♭) and C major tuning (C-G-C-G-C-E) is simply that the high E string has been lowered a half step. Therefore you must compensate accordingly. This creates a great big sound that is wonderful on 12-string guitars!

C Minor Pentatonic (C-E♭-F-G-B♭-C) - C Minor Tuning

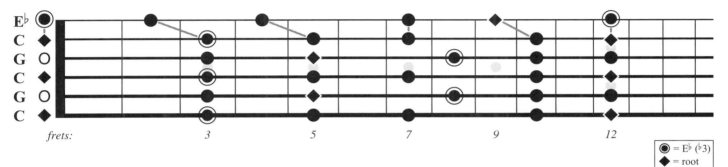

E♭
C
G
C
G
C

frets: 3 5 7 9 12

◉ = E♭ (♭3)
◆ = root

C Minor Pentatonic (C-E♭-F-G-B♭-C) - C Major Tuning

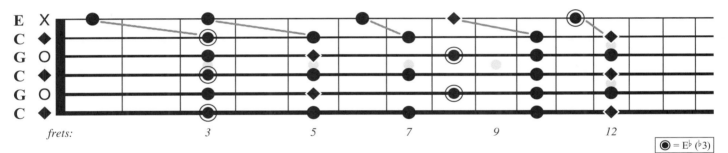

E
C
G
C
G
C

frets: 3 5 7 9 12

◉ = E♭ (♭3)

C Dorian (C-D-E♭-F-G-A-B♭-C) - C Minor Tuning B♭ Major, 2nd mode

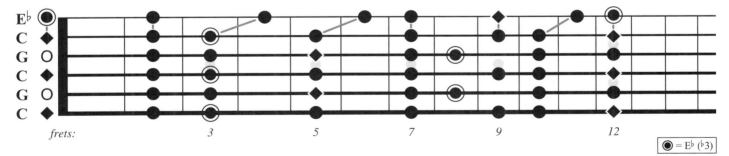

E♭
C
G
C
G
C

frets: 3 5 7 9 12

◉ = E♭ (♭3)

C Dorian (C-D-E♭-F-G-A-B♭-C) - C Major Tuning

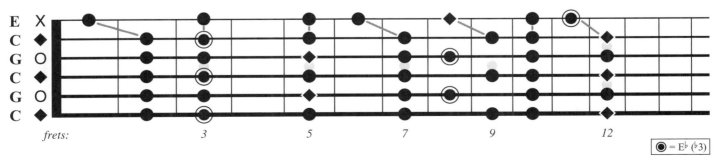

E
C
G
C
G
C

frets: 3 5 7 9 12

◉ = E♭ (♭3)

C Dorian (C–D–E♭–F–G–A–B♭–C) - C Minor Tuning B♭ Major, 2nd mode

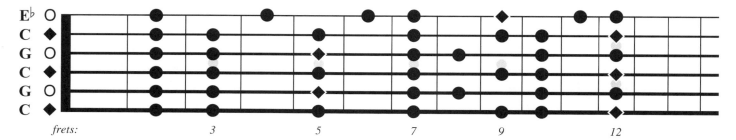

C Aeolian (C–D–E♭–F–G–A♭–B♭–C) - C Minor Tuning E♭ Major, 6th mode

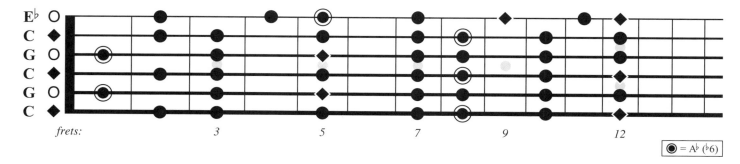

◉ = A♭ (♭6)

C Phrygian (C–D♭–E♭–F–G–A♭–B♭–C) - C Minor Tuning A♭ Major, 3rd mode

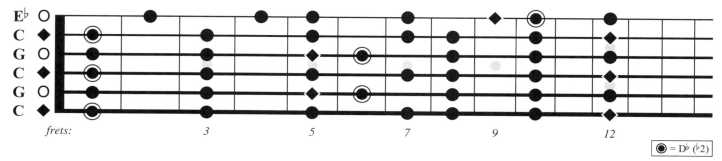

◉ = D♭ (♭2)

C Minor Song

C Minor 12-String - *C Dorian*

Open Cm Tuning:
① = E♭   ④ = C
② = C   ⑤ = G
③ = G   ⑥ = C

Track 36

56

Chapter 10

SUSPENDED TUNINGS

G Suspended

The only difference between G suspended (D-G-D-G-C-D) and G tuning (D-G-D-G-B-D) is that the B string has been raised a half step to C. This creates the suspension, and is neither minor nor major. It is similar to D-A-D-G-A-D in its tonality as there is no third present. It's great for drones and folk tunes where the third is undefined. This tuning is widely used by banjo players, who call it "mountain minor" (g-D-G-C-D). First I'll compare the G suspended and G major tunings using the minor and major pentatonic scales.

G Minor Pentatonic (G-B♭-C-D-F-G) - G Suspended Tuning

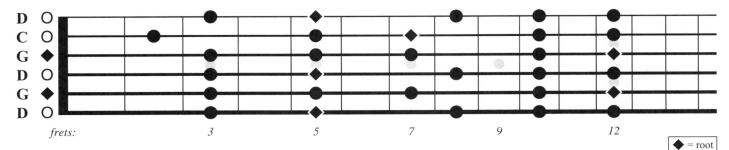

G Minor Pentatonic (G-B♭-C-D-F-G) - G Major Tuning

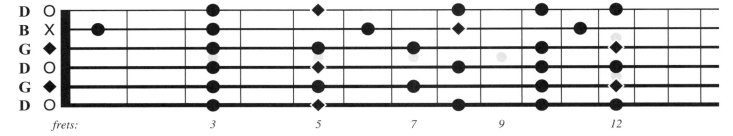

G Major Pentatonic (G-A-B-D-E-G) - G Suspended Tuning

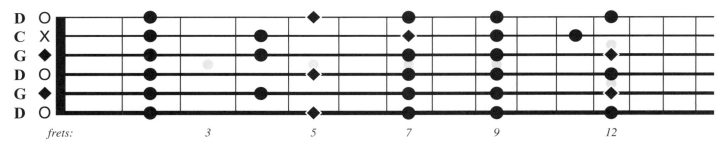

G Major Pentatonic (G-A-B-D-E-G) - G Major Tuning

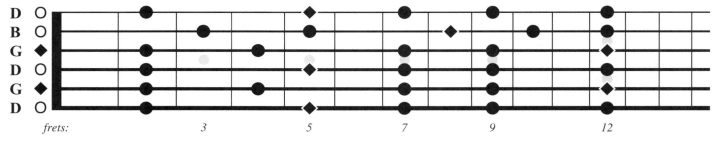

G Major (G–A–B–C–D–E–F♯–G) - G Suspended Tuning

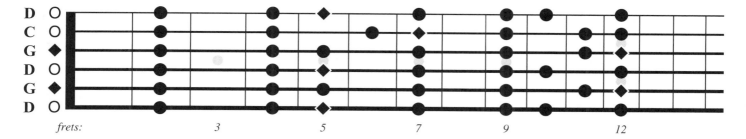

G Mixolydian (G–A–B–C–D–E–F–G) - G Suspended Tuning C Major, 5th mode

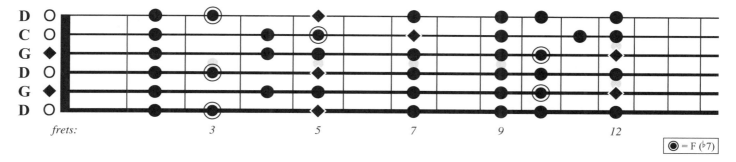

◉ = F (♭7)

G Dorian (G–A–B♭–C–D–E–F–G) - G Suspended Tuning F Major, 2nd mode

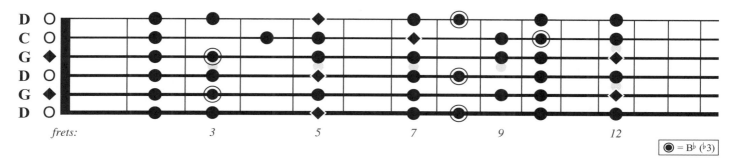

◉ = B♭ (♭3)

G Aeolian (G–A–B♭–C–D–E♭–F–G) - G Suspended Tuning B♭ Major, 6th mode

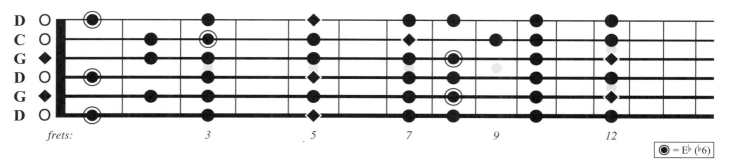

◉ = E♭ (♭6)

G Phrygian (G–A♭–B♭–C–D–E♭–F–G) - G Suspended Tuning E♭ Major, 3rd mode

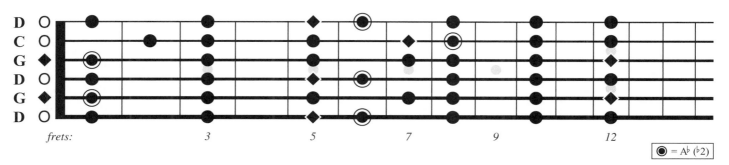

◉ = A♭ (♭2)

59

G Suspended Song

G Suspended - *G Dorian*

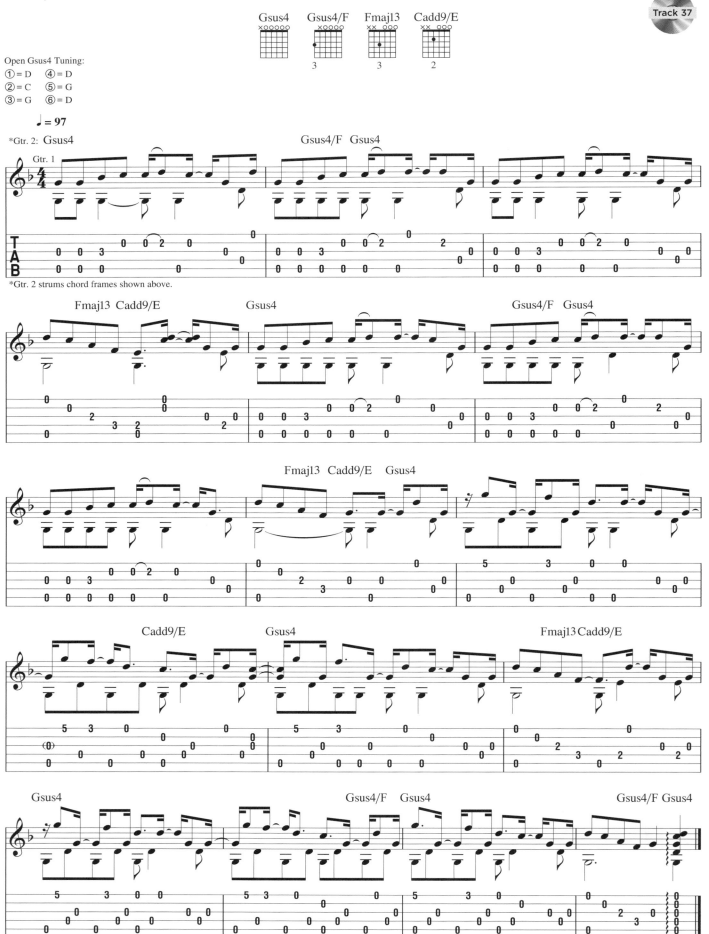

E Suspended Tuning

The only difference between this (E–B–E–A–B–E) and E tuning (E–B–E–G♯–B–E) is that the G string is raised a half step to A (from G♯).

E Minor Pentatonic (E–G–A–B–D–E) - E Suspended Tuning

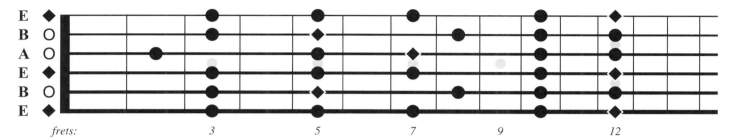

E Minor Pentatonic (E–G–A–B–D–E) - E Major Tuning

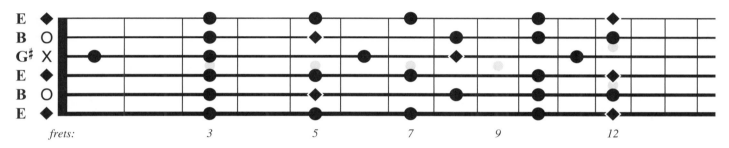

E Major Pentatonic (E–F♯–G♯–B–C♯–E) - E Suspended Tuning

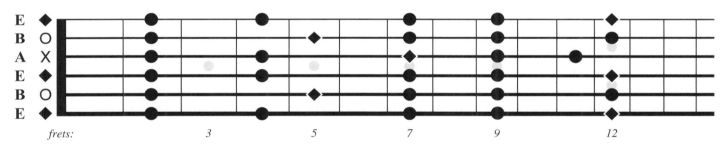

E Major Pentatonic (E–F♯–G♯–B–C♯–E) - E Major Tuning

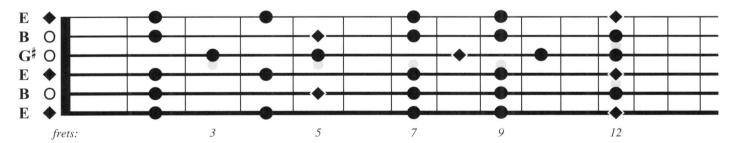

E Major (E–F♯–G♯–A–B–C♯–D–E) - E Suspended Tuning

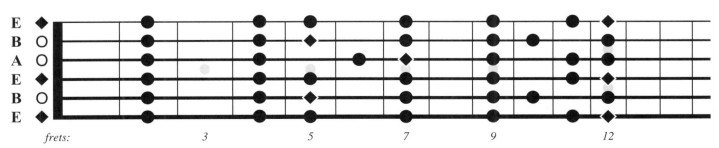

E Mixolydian (E–F#–G#–A–B–C#–D–E) - E Suspended Tuning A Major, 5th mode

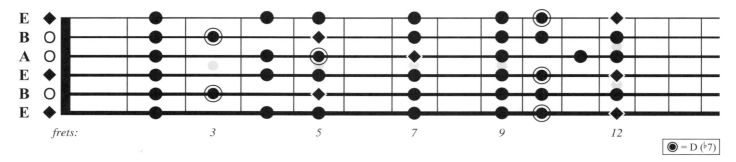

E Dorian (E–F#–G–A–B–C#–D–E) - E Suspended Tuning D Major, 2nd mode

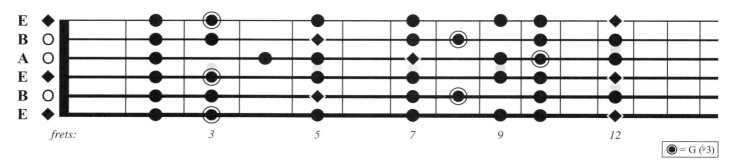

E Aeolian (E–F#–G–A–B–C–D–E) - E Suspended Tuning G Major, 6th mode

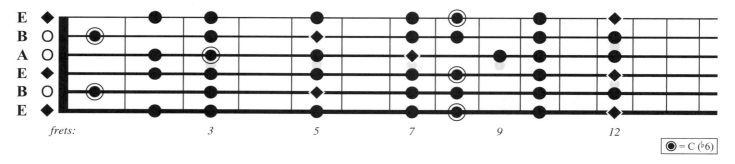

E Phrygian (E–F–G–A–B–C–D–E) - E Suspended Tuning C Major, 3rd mode

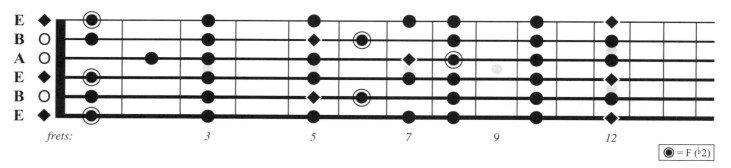

C Suspended Tuning

The difference between this (C–G–C–G–C–F) and C tuning (C–G–C–G–C–E) is that the high E string is raised a half step to F.

C Minor Pentatonic (C–E♭–F–G–B♭–C) - C Suspended Tuning

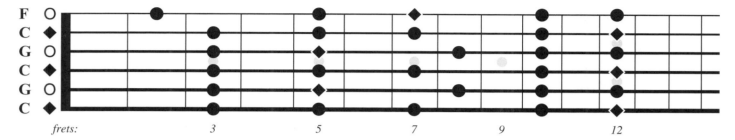

C Minor Pentatonic (C–E♭–F–G–B♭–C) - C Major Tuning

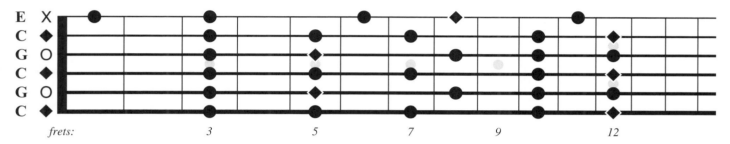

C Major Pentatonic (C–D–E–G–A–C) - C Suspended Tuning

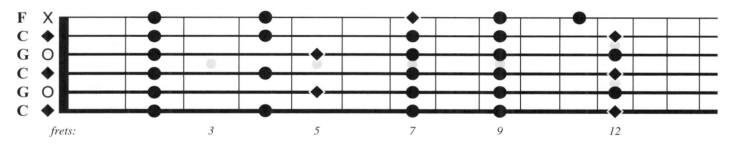

C Major Pentatonic (C–D–E–G–A–C) - C Major Tuning

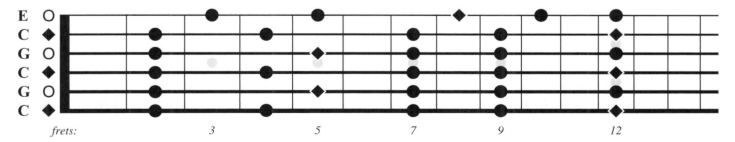

C Major (C–D–E–F–G–A–B–C) - C Suspended Tuning

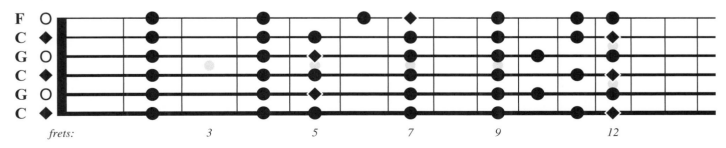

C Mixolydian (C–D–E–F–G–A–B♭–C) – C Suspended Tuning   F Major, 5th mode

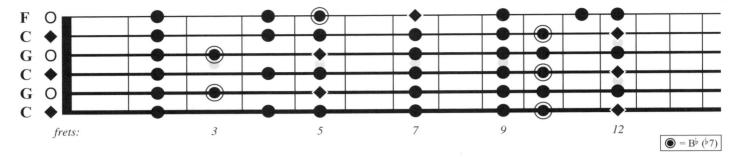

◉ = B♭ (♭7)

C Dorian (C–D–E♭–F–G–A–B♭–C) – C Suspended Tuning   B♭ Major, 2nd mode

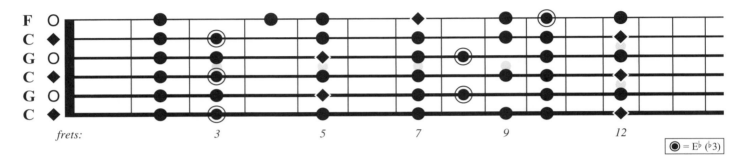

◉ = E♭ (♭3)

C Aeolian (C–D–E♭–F–G–A♭–B♭–C) – C Suspended Tuning   E♭ Major, 6th mode

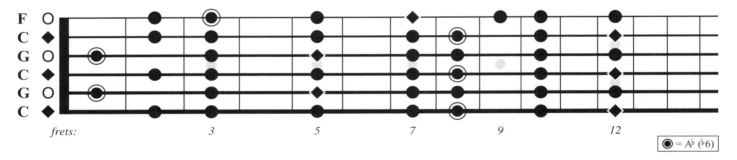

◉ = A♭ (♭6)

C Phrygian (C–D♭–E♭–F–G–A♭–B♭–C) – C Suspended Tuning   A♭ Major, 3rd mode

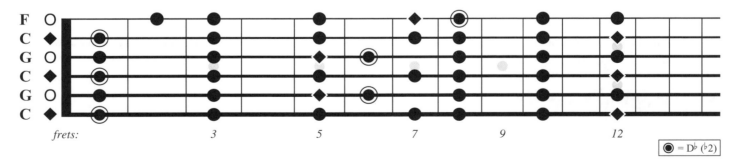

◉ = D♭ (♭2)

C Suspended 12-String - *C Mixolydian*

Open Csus4 Tuning:
①= F ④= C
②= C ⑤= G
③= G ⑥= C

Chapter 11:
UNUSUAL TUNINGS

G Sharp-Four Tuning

I devised this tuning (C#-G-C#-G-B-C#) specifically to deal with the sharp-four interval found in the Lydian and Lydian flat-seven modes. Although you can deal with this tone in a standard open tuning, I found that having the sharp four (C#) on an open string in G tuning to be more convenient for expressing the Lydian tonality. Weird but fun! Also notice that the only difference between Lydian and Lydian flat seven is the seventh tone.

G Lydian (G-A-B-C#-D-E-F#-G) - G Sharp-Four Tuning D Major, 4th mode

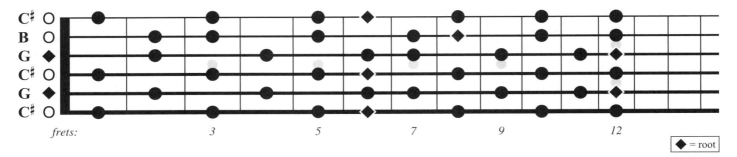

G Lydian ♭7 (G-A-B-C#-D-E-F-G) - G Sharp-Four Tuning D Melodic Minor, 4th mode

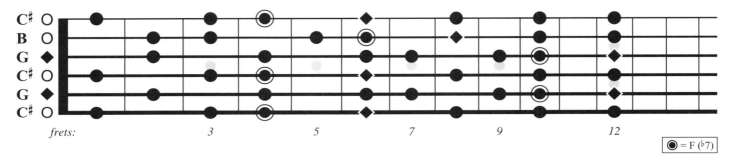

G Minor Flat-Five Tuning

This tuning (D♭-G-D♭-G-B♭-D♭) is specifically designed to express the Locrian mode. The only differences between it and G sharp-four tuning are the enharmonic changes between C# and D♭ (which, of course, are the same note) and the B string has been lowered a half step to B♭ to make the tonality minor.

G Locrian (G-A♭-B♭-C-D♭-E♭-F-G) - G Flat-Five Tuning A♭ Major, 7th mode

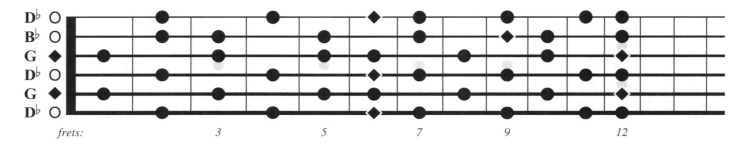

E Sharp-Four Tuning

E Lydian (E–F#–G#–A#–B–C#–D#–E) - E Sharp-Four Tuning B Major, 4th mode

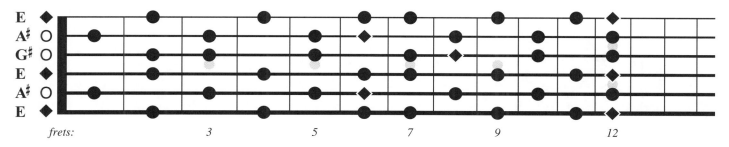

E Lydian ♭7 (E–F#–G#–A#–B–C#–D–E) - E Sharp-Four Tuning B Melodic Minor, 4th mode

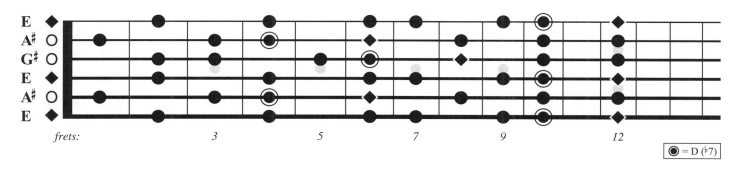

◉ = D (♭7)

E Minor Flat-Five Tuning

E Locrian (E–F–G–A–B♭–C–D–E) - E Minor Flat-Five Tuning F Major, 7th mode

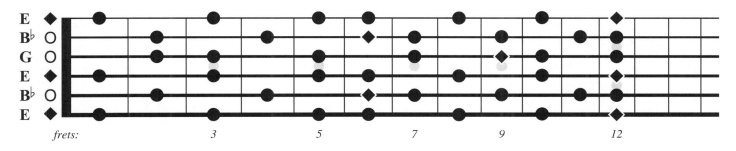

G Sharp-Four Song - *G Lydian*

Track 39

Open G(#4) Tuning:
① = C#   ④ = C#
② = B   ⑤ = G
③ = G   ⑥ = C#

Freely ♩ = 110

68

E Minor 11 Tuning

This tuning (E–B–D–G–A–D) is David Crosby world—dreamy and evocative. Check out how lovely the harmonics ring. A thing of beauty! Keep in mind that the fifth string is now a B, the second string is A, and the high E string is tuned down to D. It is D–A–D–G–A–D on the top four strings and E tuning on the bottom two, making it superb for droning.

E Minor Pentatonic (E–G–A–B–D–E) - E Minor 11 Tuning

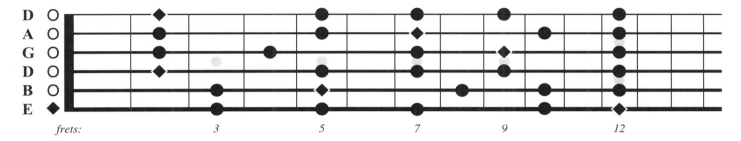

E Dorian (E–F♯–G–A–B–C♯–D–E) - E Minor 11 Tuning D Major, 2nd mode

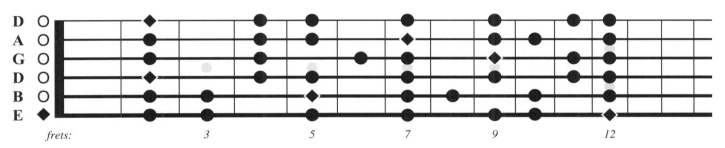

E Aeolian (E–F♯–G–A–B–C–D–E) - E Minor 11 Tuning G Major, 6th mode

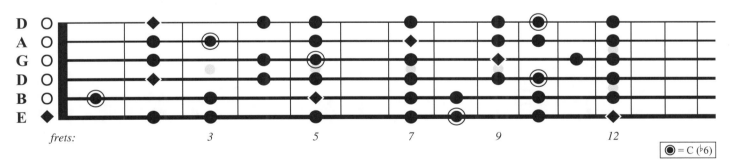

◉ = C (♭6)

E Phrygian (E–F–G–A–B–C–D–E) - E Minor 11 Tuning C Major, 3rd mode

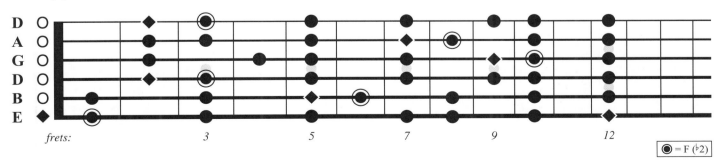

◉ = F (♭2)

E Minor 11 Song - *E Aeolian*

Open Em11 Tuning:

① = D ④ = D
② = A ⑤ = B
③ = G ⑥ = E

♩ = 114

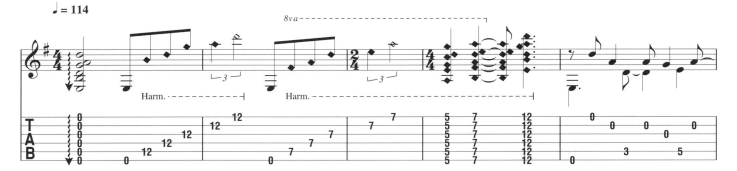

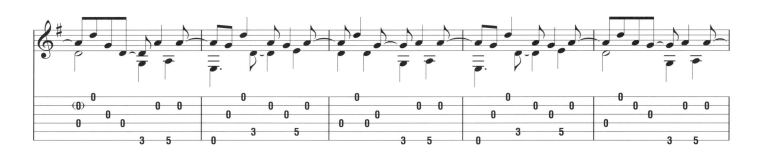

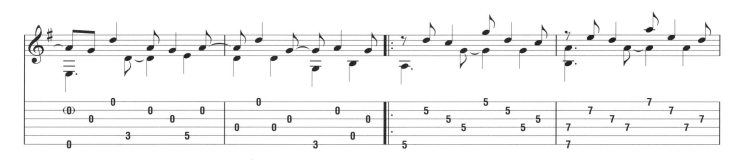

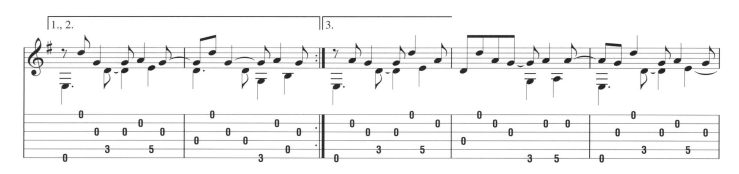

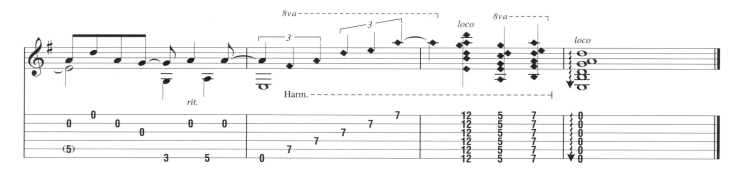

C Wahine Tuning

A Wahine tuning is any tuning containing a major seventh interval. There are many variations, and you could easily spend years on this family of tunings alone and be quite busy and inspired. This C Wahine example is G tuning (D–G–D–G–B–D) with the sixth string tuned down to C. This enables you to expand the low range and play in the key of C more comfortably. I like to play in G Mixolydian on the top five strings and resolve to C tonality by including the low sixth string (retuned to C) and playing a C chord on the top five strings. There is much joy and beauty to be discovered here—it is a tranquil and pleasant place to improvise. The B string is now the major-seventh tone, and this leads to the enjoyment of the key of C major. Listening to anything by Hawaiian masters Leonard Kwan and Keola Beamer will help your troubles dissolve into beauty.

C Major (C–D–E–F–G–A–B–C) - C Wahine Tuning

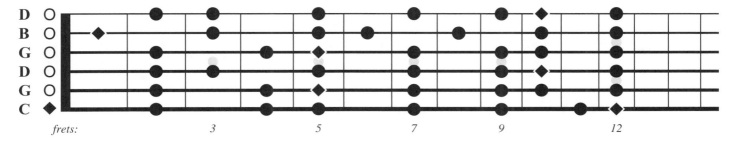

G Mixolydian (G–A–B–C–D–E–F–G) - C Wahine Tuning

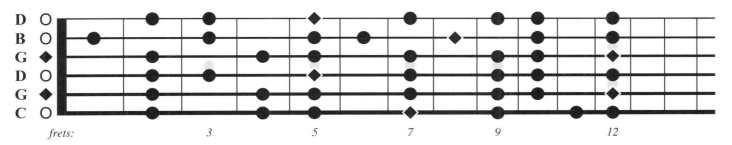

G Mixolydian - G Tuning

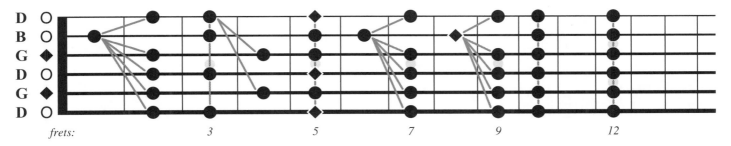

C Wahine Song - *C Major*

Chapter 12:

COMMON BONDS

G, E, and C Major Tunings

This chapter illustrates the common bonds shared by G, E, and C tunings. See how the web of lines shifts from the B string (in G tuning), to the G string (in E tuning), to the high E string (in C tuning). The lines originate from the pivot string which is tuned to the third of each respective open tuning. There is the magic tonal combination of three strings, tuned fifth-root-third, to be found in each tuning. In G tuning, it's the D–G–B strings; in E tuning, the B–E–G♯ strings; and in C tuning: the G–C–E strings.

G Major (G-A-B-C-D-E-F♯-G) - G Tuning

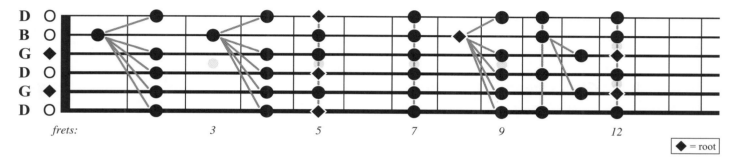

◆ = root

E Major (E-F♯-G♯-A-B-C♯-D♯-E) - E Tuning

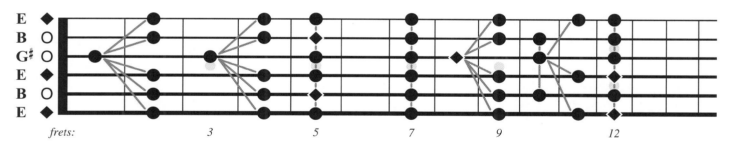

C Major (C-D-E-F-G-A-B-C) - C Tuning

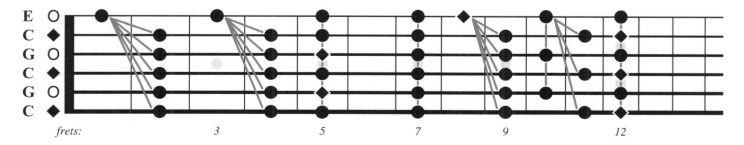

In G tuning the D, G, and B strings are unaltered. They exist in the same shapes as standard tuning. If you know how to negotiate these three strings in standard tuning, you can apply that knowledge to the trio of like intervals in all three tunings. Remember: the fifth, root, and third shapes all stay the same in these three tunings, they just shift to different strings.

Three-String Examples

E Tuning Three-String Grouping - *E Major*

Open E Tuning:
①= E ④= E
②= B ⑤= B
③= G♯ ⑥= E

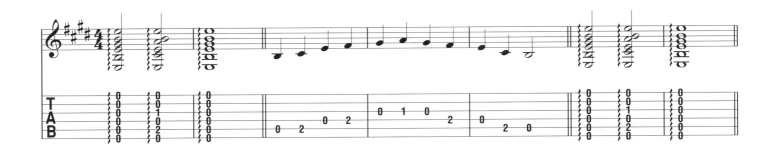

G Tuning Three-String Grouping - *G Major*

Open G Tuning:
①= D ④= D
②= B ⑤= G
③= G ⑥= D

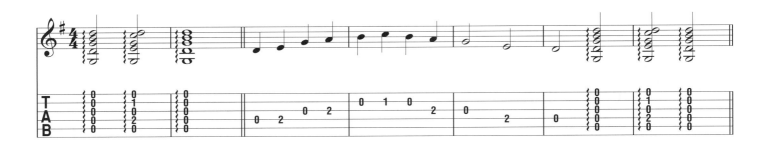

C Tuning Three-String Grouping - *C Major*

Open C Tuning:
①= E ④= C
②= C ⑤= G
③= G ⑥= C

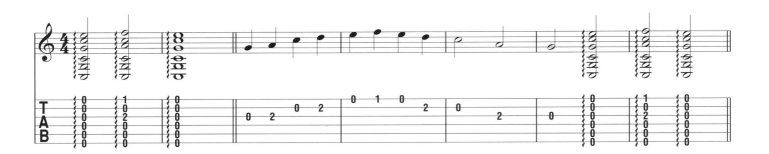

Three-String Songs

E Tuning - *E Major*

Track 45

Open E Tuning:
①= E ④= E
②= B ⑤= B
③= G# ⑥= E

♩ = 100

*Two gtrs. arr. for one.

G Tuning - *G Major*

Open G Tuning:
①= D ④= D
②= B ⑤= G
③= G ⑥= D

♩ = 100

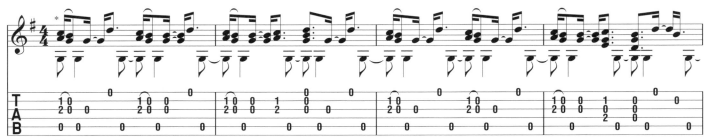

*Two gtrs. arr. for one.

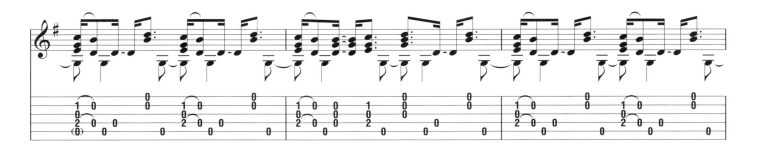

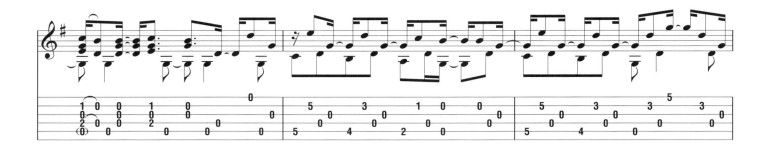

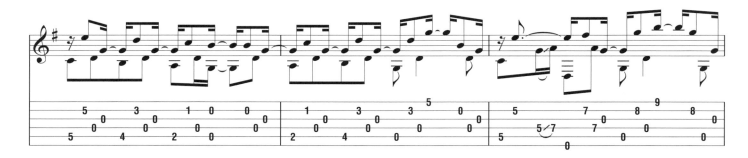

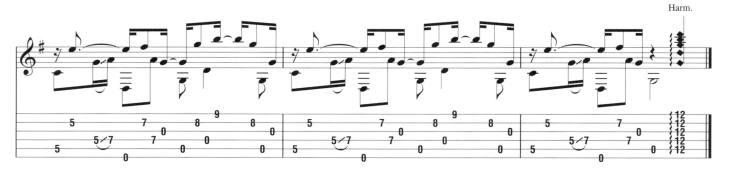

C Tuning - *C Major*

Open C Tuning:
①= E ④= C
②= C ⑤= G
③= G ⑥= C

*Two gtrs. arr. for one.

Mixolydian Mode

Notice how in Mixolydian mode, the spiderweb shapes originate at the fifth fret. In G tuning, C major starts at the fifth fret; in E tuning, A major starts at the fifth fret; and in C tuning, F major starts at the fifth fret. Keep this in mind when using a capo in any of these tunings.

G Mixolydian (G–A–B–C–D–E–F–G) - G Tuning C Major, 5th mode

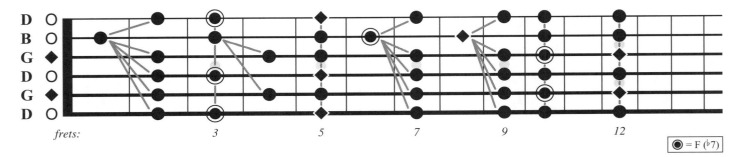

E Mixolydian (E–F♯–G♯–A–B–C♯–D–E) - E Tuning A Major, 5th mode

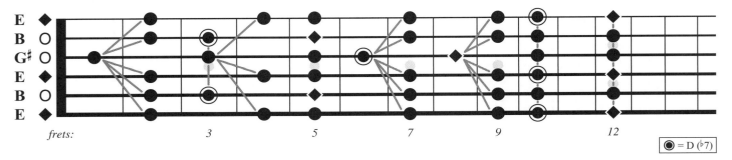

C Mixolydian (C–D–E–F–G–A–B♭–C) - C Tuning F Major, 5th mode

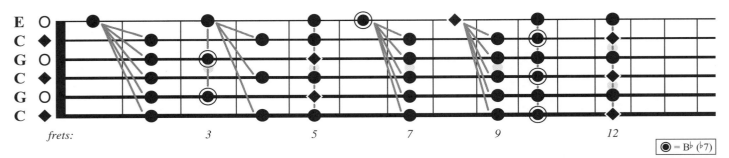

Dropped D and Double Dropped D

Dropped D (D-A-D-G-B-E) is simply standard tuning with the low E string lowered to D. This expands the range and enables you to easily play in D. Taj Mahal opened this door for me, and Stephen Stills pushed me through! Double dropped D (D-A-D-G-B-D) also expands the range and allows you to drone the high first string (lowered to D). You can still think standard tuning on the inside four strings. Neil Young's "Cinnamon Girl" says it all.

D Major (D-E-F♯-G-A-B-C♯-D) - Drop D Tuning

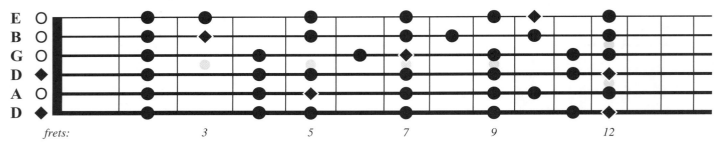

78

D Major - Standard Tuning

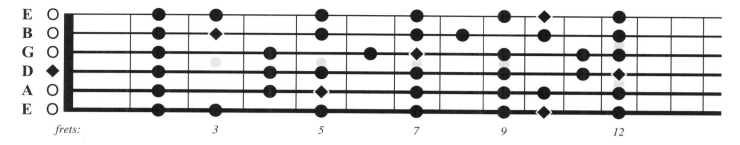

D Major - Double Drop D Tuning

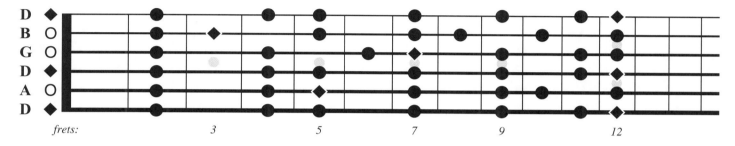

D Major - Standard Tuning

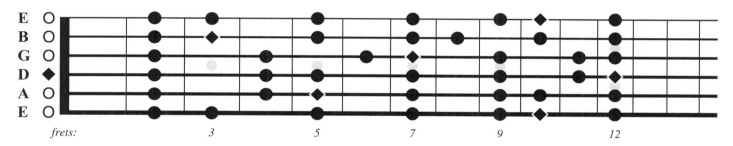

D Minor Pentatonic (D-F-G-A-C-D) - Drop D Tuning

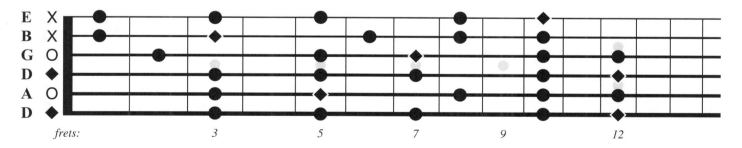

D Minor Pentatonic - Standard Tuning

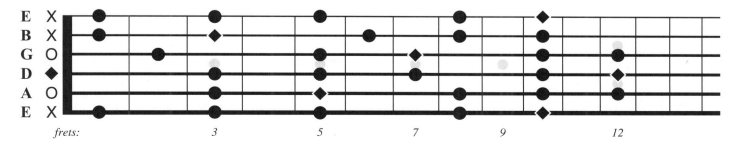

D Minor Pentatonic - Double Drop D Tuning

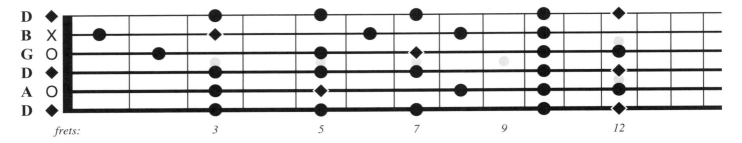

D Minor Pentatonic - Standard Tuning

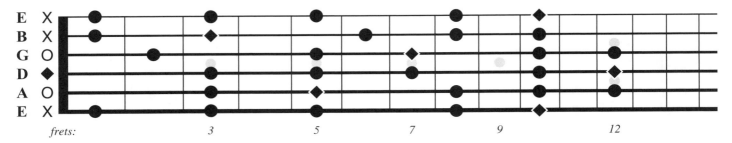

Double Dropped D Song

Double Dropped D - *D Major*

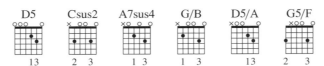

Double Drop D Tuning:
① = D   ④ = D
② = B   ⑤ = A
③ = G   ⑥ = D

♩ = 96

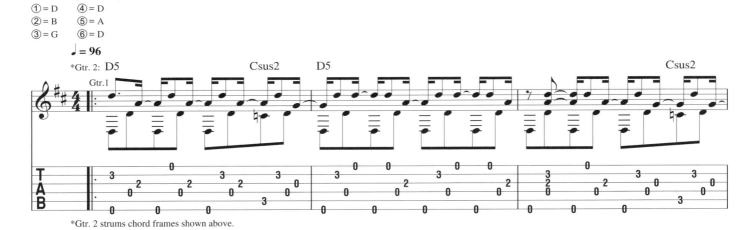

*Gtr. 2 strums chord frames shown above.

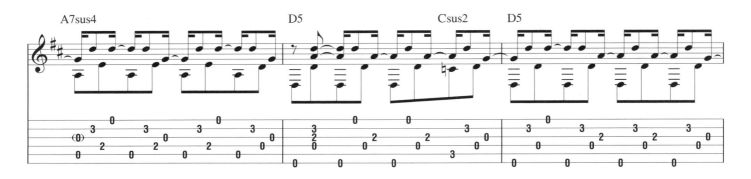

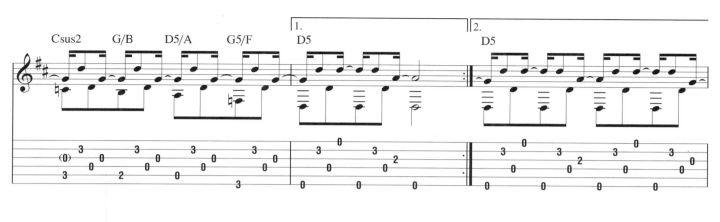

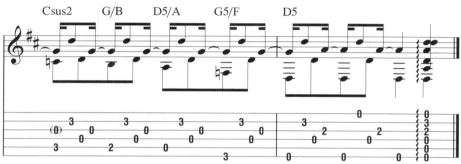

Drone Tunings

D–A–D–D–A–D is a drone tuning with just roots and fifths. It is very dulcimer like and provides a dreamy landscape. It's also fun to play slide in. Check out Ben Harper's mastery of this tuning.

D Major Pentatonic (D-E-F♯-A-B-D) - D-A-D-D-A-D Tuning

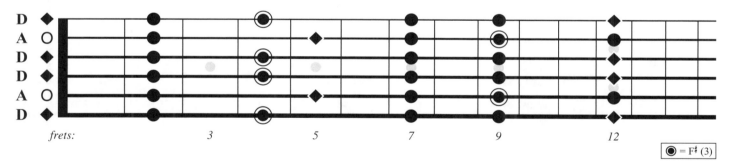

D Minor Pentatonic (D-F-G-A-C-D) - D-A-D-D-A-D Tuning

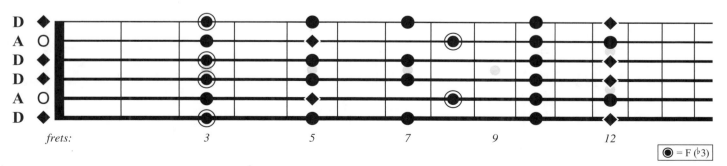

G–G–D–G–G–D is constructed on the same principle as D–A–D–D–A–D but there is a different placement of intervals. It's great for drones à la Daniel Lanois.

G Major Pentatonic (G-A-B-D-E-G) - G-G-D-G-G-D Tuning

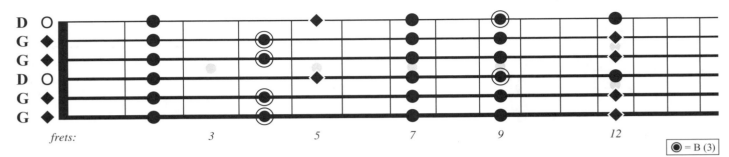

G Minor Pentatonic (G-B♭-C-D-F-G) - G-G-D-G-G-D Tuning

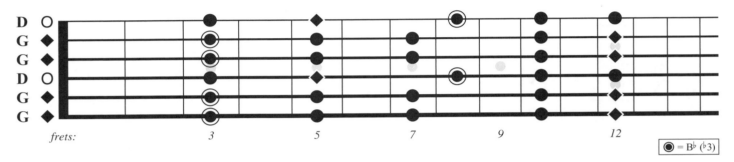

Drone Tuning Songs

D–A–D–D–A–D Minor Slide - *D Minor Pentatonic*

Track 49

D-A-D-D-A-D Tuning:
① = D ④ = D
② = A ⑤ = A
③ = D ⑥ = D

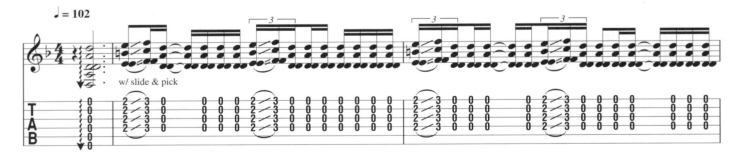

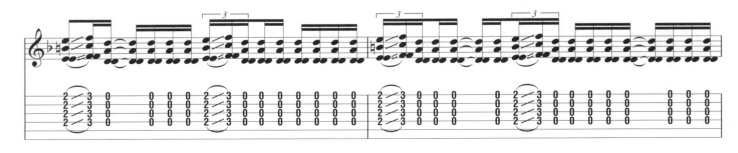

G-G-D-G-G-D - *G Major Pentatonic*

① = D ④ = D
② = G ⑤ = G
③ = G ⑥ = G

84

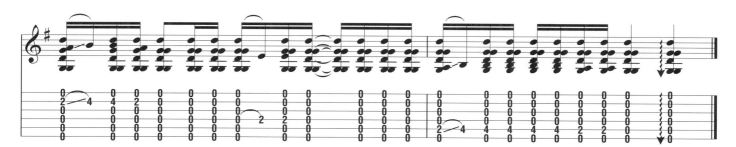

G Minor Drone - *G Minor Pentatonic*

① = D ④ = D
② = G ⑤ = G
③ = G ⑥ = G

♩ = 92

Chapter 13:
LYDIAN AND LOCRIAN MODES

I don't play in these modes as much as I do in other modes of the major scale, but I have included them here for the sake of completeness. That being said, there are great possibilities here for striking tonalities that interest the ear and are worthy of being explored. Notice that the only difference between the major scale and the Lydian mode is the sharp-four interval; the only difference between Lydian and Lydian flat-seven is the flat-seven interval; and the only difference between Lydian flat-seven and Mixolydian is the sharp-four interval.

Standard Tuning

C Major (C–D–E–F–G–A–B–C) - Standard Tuning

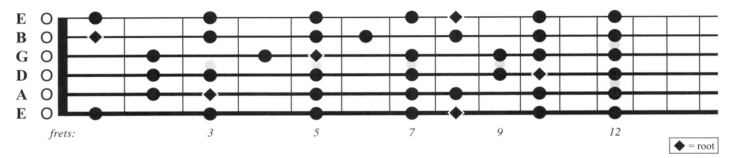

◆ = root

C Lydian (C–D–E–F♯–G–A–B–C) - Standard Tuning G Major, 4th mode

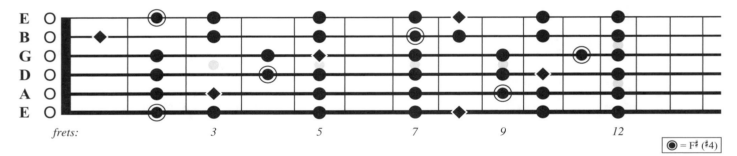

◉ = F♯ (♯4)

C Lydian ♭7 (C–D–E–F♯–G–A–B♭–C) - Standard Tuning G Melodic Minor, 4th mode

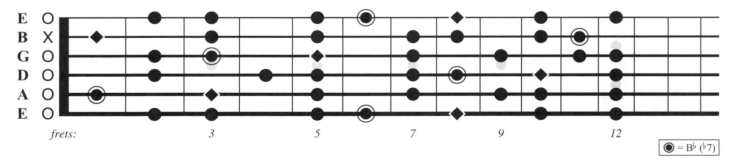

◉ = B♭ (♭7)

C Locrian (C–D♭–E♭–F–G♭–A♭–B♭–C) - Standard Tuning D♭ Major, 7th mode

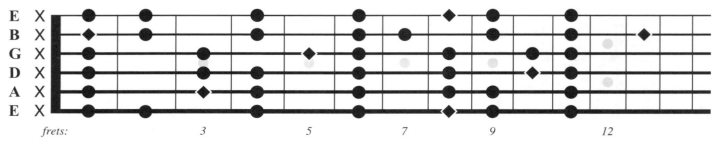

G Tuning

G Major (G–A–B–C–D–E–F♯–G) - G Tuning

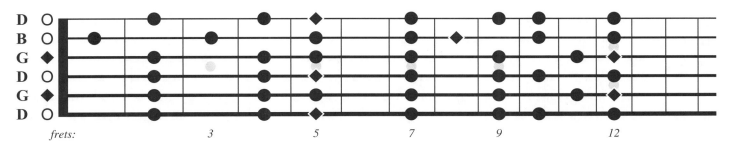

G Lydian (G–A–B–C♯–D–E–F♯–G) - G Tuning D Major, 4th mode

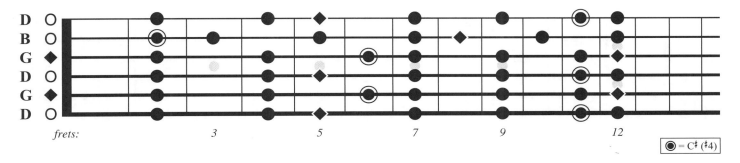

◉ = C♯ (♯4)

G Lydian ♭7 (G–A–B–C♯–D–E–F–G) - G Tuning D Melodic Minor, 4th mode

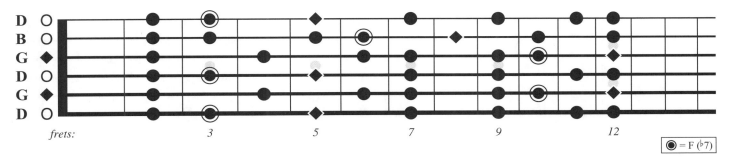

◉ = F (♭7)

G Mixolydian (G–A–B–C–D–E–F–G) - G Tuning C Major, 5th mode

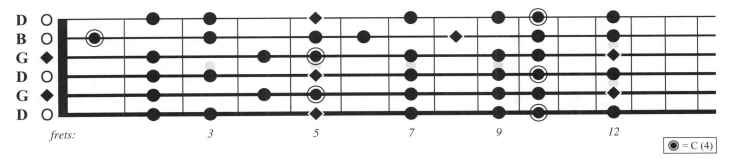

◉ = C (4)

E Tuning

E Major (E-F#-G#-A-B-C#-D#-E) - E Tuning

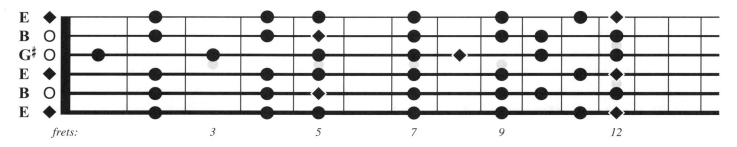

E Lydian (E-F#-G#-A#-B-C#-D#-E) - E Tuning B Major, 4th mode

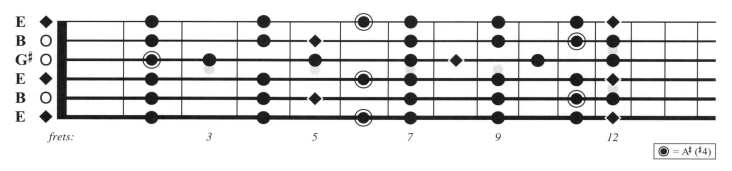

◉ = A# (#4)

E Lydian ♭7 (E-F#-G#-A#-B-C#-D-E) - E Tuning B Melodic Minor, 4th mode

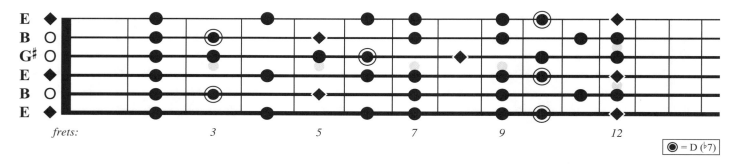

◉ = D (♭7)

E Mixolydian (E-F#-G#-A-B-C#-D-E) - E Tuning A Major, 5th mode

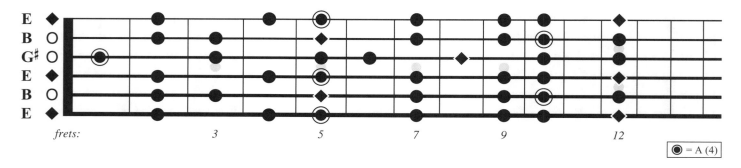

◉ = A (4)

C Tuning

C Major (C–D–E–F–G–A–B–C) – C Tuning

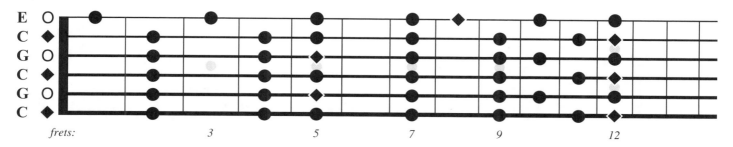

C Lydian (C–D–E–F♯–G–A–B–C) – C Tuning G Major, 4th mode

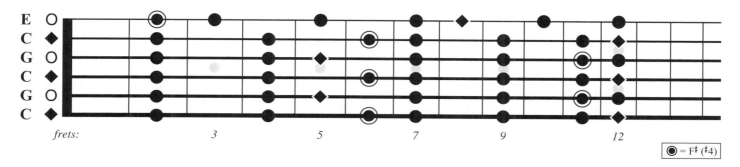

◉ = F♯ (♯4)

C Lydian ♭7 (C–D–E–F♯–G–A–B♭–C) – C Tuning G Melodic Minor, 4th mode

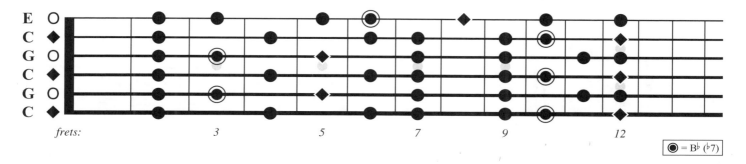

◉ = B♭ (♭7)

C Mixolydian (C–D–E–F–G–A–B♭–C) – C Tuning F Major, 5th mode

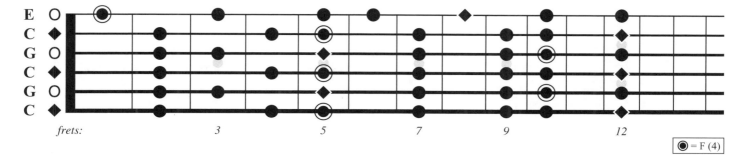

◉ = F (4)

C Locrian (C–D♭–E♭–F–G♭–A♭–B♭–C) – C Tuning D♭ Major, 7th mode

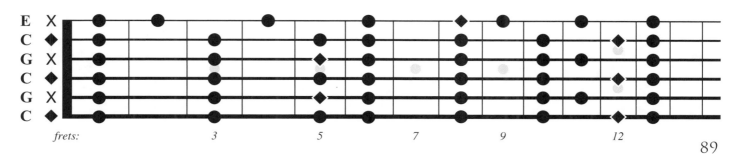

89

G Lydian Song

G Lydian

Open G Tuning:
①= D   ④= D
②= B   ⑤= G
③= G   ⑥= D

Freely ♩= 86

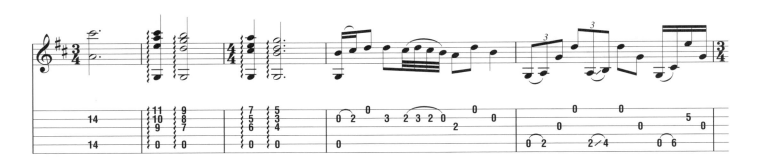

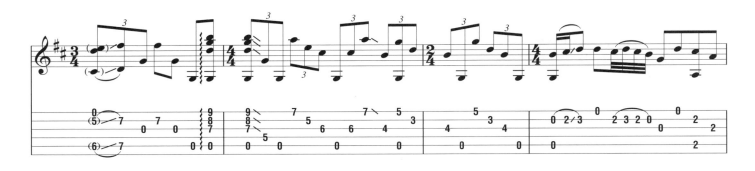

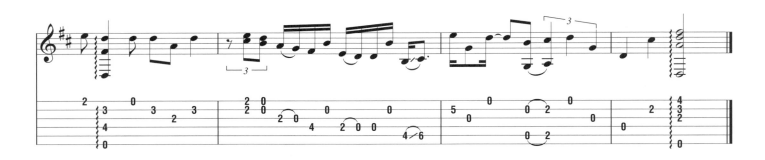

AFTERWORD

"Two roads diverged in a yellow wood..." and so begins the journey of a thousand miles. It is my hope that this book has helped illuminate the road less traveled, and given you a newfound understanding of and appreciation for the seemingly endless possibilities that exist around us. The tunings analyzed in this book are important and frequently used, however, many more exist than I could possibly illustrate here.

I encourage you to continue your own explorations. For truly ground-breaking work listen to artists such as Michael Hedges, Joni Mitchell, David Crosby, and Pierre Bensusan. They are masters at creating, harnessing, and adapting tunings to express something unique and beautiful. Using a specific tuning designed to express a certain tonality is indeed a formidable tool for every guitarist. The range and palette of colors provided by alternate tunings are unsurpassed in tonal complexity, depth, and variation. Endless amounts of beauty, emotion, and mystery wait patiently for you to unlock and explore. And I hope you do each and every time you pick up your guitar. Way leads onto way.

Peace and gratitude,
Mark Shark

ACKNOWLEDGMENTS

This book came about as a series of fortunate events I feel compelled to address. Throughout my career I have been blessed, inspired, and challenged by key masters and students who have knowingly, or unknowingly, provided the catalyst by which this work exists. Your presence in my life has made all the difference... "thank you" hardly seems enough.

For the artists in this book, particularly Jesse Ed Davis, Bonnie Raitt, and Jackson Browne, and all of the monstrously talented musicians out there on the road, endlessly gigging and making it happen, see you soon; for Richard Tao, whose inspiration, advice, friendship, and generosity has proven invaluable to me while creating this book; for Tim Wingate and James Needham for their superior and tireless efforts in assisting Richard and I with the many drawings and transcriptions represented here; for Randall Wixen and Jeff Schroedl for taking the time and being real; for Kurt Plahna and all the good folks at Hal Leonard for their formidable efforts in editing and design; for Doug Niedt, Jerry Hahn, and Bill Schatzkamer whose early influence and stunning talent still inspire me; for Wyn Davis and Mike Sutherland of Total Access for their great ears; for Graffitiman (a.k.a. John Trudell and Bad Dog) for all those years; for my four beautiful sisters, Laura, Nina, Kyriena, and Helena; and of course to all the rest of the Schatzkamer-Sedaka clan... more than you know.

Thanks and gratitude to Buddha and Cree Miller, Kathy Kane, Jamaica Raphael, Joel Raphael, Paul Dieter, Groovemasters, Gibson, Fender, and Goodall Guitars, Roland, ASCAP, Pete Seeger, Chuck Berry, Debashis Bhattacharya, Scott Summerville, Hutch Hutchison, James Cruce, Byron Berline, Ulali, Floyd Westerman, Kelly Ed Davis, Taj Mahal, Bob Dylan, George Harrison, John Fogerty, Hani Naser, Betty Billups, Quiltman, Little Steven, Pat McDonald, Indigo Girls, Faye Brown, Johnny Lee Schell, Tony Braunagel, Amy Nelson and Cathy Guthrie of Folk Uke, Danny Timms, Teresa James, Terry Wilson, Billy Watts, Jerry Peterson, Debra Dobkin, Tony Zamora, Jennifer Warnes, David Jackson, Kris Kristofferson, Willie Nelson, Gary Ray, Bobby Tsukamoto, Dave Melton, Kirk Fletcher, Gary Ferguson, Terry Evans, Phil Bloch, Mark Goldberg, Pete Fahey, Stephen Hodges, John Bazz, Keith Wyatt, Doug Legacy, Van Dyke Parks, Wally Ingram, Eddie Batos, Jorge Calderon, Todd Robinson, Skip Edwards, Mark Browne, Tony Gilkyson, Freebo, Gina French, Catfish Hodge, Jeff Steele, Lisa Haley, Billy Block, Rip Masters, Jimmy Harris, Ken O'Malley, Will McGregor, Dillon O'Brian, Dean Parks, Jodi Siegal, Jimmy Z, George Safire, Bob Wagstaff, Rhythm and Notes Music, Mark Fitchett, the Guitar School, Ricky Eckstein, Carol Eckstein, Alan Singer, West LA Studio Services, Glen Nishida, Pacifica Studios, Colin Blair, Music Folk, Sergio and crew of Blue Sky Productions, Gordon and Cary Bland, Bill Costello, Bill Engel, Glen Harris, Farshid Etniko, Benet Schaeffer, Brian Casserly, Tom Maloney, Matt Murdick, KDHX, Elliot Goldberg, Barie Joy, Roy Mendelsohn, Linda James, Dale Stuart, the Bland family, Costello family, Dawson family, Eckstein family, Engel family, Erilane family, Ferguson family, Goldsmith family, Marsh family, O'Neal family, Robinson family, Sabatino family, Sahme family, Tao family, Treman-Riblett family, Trudell family, Virga-Costa family, Watts family, and Welch family—your love and support is cherished and sustaining—and last but not least, for my own beautiful family Dylan, Shiloh, and Robin... this wouldn't exist without you.

THE TAO OF TUNINGS CD TRACK LIST

GUITAR NOTATION LEGEND

Guitar music can be notated three different ways: on a *musical staff*, in *tablature*, and in *rhythm slashes*.

RHYTHM SLASHES are written above the staff. Strum chords in the rhythm indicated. Use the chord diagrams found at the top of the first page of the transcription for the appropriate chord voicings. Round noteheads indicate single notes.

THE MUSICAL STAFF shows pitches and rhythms and is divided by bar lines into measures. Pitches are named after the first seven letters of the alphabet.

TABLATURE graphically represents the guitar fingerboard. Each horizontal line represents a string, and each number represents a fret.

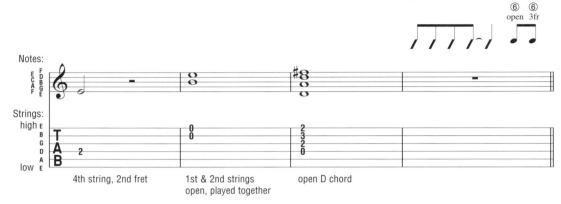

4th string, 2nd fret   1st & 2nd strings open, played together   open D chord

DEFINITIONS FOR SPECIAL GUITAR NOTATION

HALF-STEP BEND: Strike the note and bend up 1/2 step.

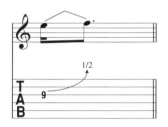

WHOLE-STEP BEND: Strike the note and bend up one step.

GRACE NOTE BEND: Strike the note and immediately bend up as indicated.

SLIGHT (MICROTONE) BEND: Strike the note and bend up 1/4 step.

BEND AND RELEASE: Strike the note and bend up as indicated, then release back to the original note. Only the first note is struck.

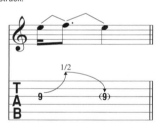

PRE-BEND: Bend the note as indicated, then strike it.

PRE-BEND AND RELEASE: Bend the note as indicated. Strike it and release the bend back to the original note.

UNISON BEND: Strike the two notes simultaneously and bend the lower note up to the pitch of the higher.

VIBRATO: The string is vibrated by rapidly bending and releasing the note with the fretting hand.

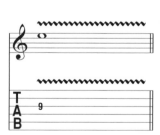

WIDE VIBRATO: The pitch is varied to a greater degree by vibrating with the fretting hand.

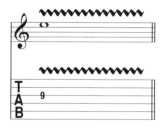

HAMMER-ON: Strike the first (lower) note with one finger, then sound the higher note (on the same string) with another finger by fretting it without picking.

PULL-OFF: Place both fingers on the notes to be sounded. Strike the first note and without picking, pull the finger off to sound the second (lower) note.

LEGATO SLIDE: Strike the first note and then slide the same fret-hand finger up or down to the second note. The second note is not struck.

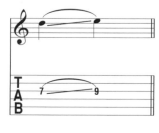

SHIFT SLIDE: Same as legato slide, except the second note is struck.

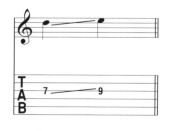

TRILL: Very rapidly alternate between the notes indicated by continuously hammering on and pulling off.

TAPPING: Hammer ("tap") the fret indicated with the pick-hand index or middle finger and pull off to the note fretted by the fret hand.

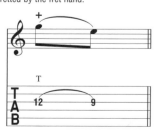

NATURAL HARMONIC: Strike the note while the fret-hand lightly touches the string directly over the fret indicated.

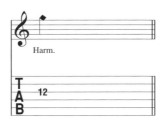

Harm.

PINCH HARMONIC: The note is fretted normally and a harmonic is produced by adding the edge of the thumb or the tip of the index finger of the pick hand to the normal pick attack.

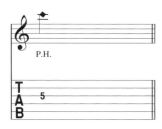

P.H.

HARP HARMONIC: The note is fretted normally and a harmonic is produced by gently resting the pick hand's index finger directly above the indicated fret (in parentheses) while the pick hand's thumb or pick assists by plucking the appropriate string.

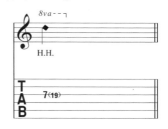

H.H.

PICK SCRAPE: The edge of the pick is rubbed down (or up) the string, producing a scratchy sound.

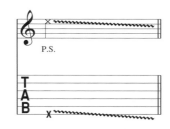

P.S.

MUFFLED STRINGS: A percussive sound is produced by laying the fret hand across the string(s) without depressing, and striking them with the pick hand.

PALM MUTING: The note is partially muted by the pick hand lightly touching the string(s) just before the bridge.

P.M.

RAKE: Drag the pick across the strings indicated with a single motion.

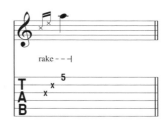

rake

TREMOLO PICKING: The note is picked as rapidly and continuously as possible.

ARPEGGIATE: Play the notes of the chord indicated by quickly rolling them from bottom to top.

VIBRATO BAR DIVE AND RETURN: The pitch of the note or chord is dropped a specified number of steps (in rhythm), then returned to the original pitch.

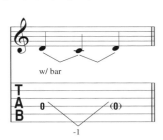

w/ bar

VIBRATO BAR SCOOP: Depress the bar just before striking the note, then quickly release the bar.

w/ bar

VIBRATO BAR DIP: Strike the note and then immediately drop a specified number of steps, then release back to the original pitch.

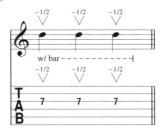

w/ bar

ADDITIONAL MUSICAL DEFINITIONS

 (accent) • Accentuate note (play it louder).

 (accent) • Accentuate note with great intensity.

 (staccato) • Play the note short.

 • Downstroke

V • Upstroke

D.S. al Coda • Go back to the sign (𝄋), then play until the measure marked "***To Coda***," then skip to the section labelled "**Coda**."

D.C. al Fine • Go back to the beginning of the song and play until the measure marked "***Fine***" (end).

Rhy. Fig. • Label used to recall a recurring accompaniment pattern (usually chordal).

Riff • Label used to recall composed, melodic lines (usually single notes) which recur.

Fill • Label used to identify a brief melodic figure which is to be inserted into the arrangement.

Rhy. Fill • A chordal version of a Fill.

tacet • Instrument is silent (drops out).

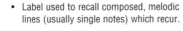 • Repeat measures between signs.

  • When a repeated section has different endings, play the first ending only the first time and the second ending only the second time.

NOTE: Tablature numbers in parentheses mean:
1. The note is being sustained over a system (note in standard notation is tied), or
2. The note is sustained, but a new articulation (such as a hammer-on, pull-off, slide or vibrato) begins, or
3. The note is a barely audible "ghost" note (note in standard notation is also in parentheses).

Get Better at Guitar

...with these Great Guitar Instruction Books from Hal Leonard!

101 GUITAR TIPS
STUFF ALL THE PROS KNOW AND USE
by Adam St. James
This book contains invaluable guidance on everything from scales and music theory to truss rod adjustments, proper recording studio set-ups, and much more. The book also features snippets of advice from some of the most celebrated guitarists and producers in the music business, including B.B. King, Steve Vai, Joe Satriani, Warren Haynes, Laurence Juber, Pete Anderson, Tom Dowd and others, culled from the author's hundreds of interviews.
00695737 Book/CD Pack.........................$16.95

AMAZING PHRASING
50 WAYS TO IMPROVE YOUR IMPROVISATIONAL SKILLS
by Tom Kolb
This book/CD pack explores all the main components necessary for crafting well-balanced rhythmic and melodic phrases. It also explains how these phrases are put together to form cohesive solos. Many styles are covered – rock, blues, jazz, fusion, country, Latin, funk and more – and all of the concepts are backed up with musical examples. The companion CD contains 89 demos for listening, and most tracks feature full-band backing.
00695583 Book/CD Pack.........................$19.95

BLUES YOU CAN USE
by John Ganapes
A comprehensive source designed to help guitarists develop both lead and rhythm playing. Covers: Texas, Delta, R&B, early rock and roll, gospel, blues/rock and more. Includes: 21 complete solos • chord progressions and riffs • turnarounds • moveable scales and more. CD features leads and full band backing.
00695007 Book/CD Pack.........................$19.95

FRETBOARD MASTERY
by Troy Stetina
Untangle the mysterious regions of the guitar fretboard and unlock your potential. *Fretboard Mastery* familiarizes you with all the shapes you need to know by applying them in real musical examples, thereby reinforcing and reaffirming your newfound knowledge. The result is a much higher level of comprehension and retention.
00695331 Book/CD Pack.........................$19.95

FRETBOARD ROADMAPS – 2ND EDITION
ESSENTIAL GUITAR PATTERNS THAT ALL THE PROS KNOW AND USE
by Fred Sokolow
The updated edition of this bestseller features more songs, updated lessons, and a full audio CD! Learn to play lead and rhythm anywhere on the fretboard, in any key; play a variety of lead guitar styles; play chords and progressions anywhere on the fretboard; expand your chord vocabulary; and learn to think musically – the way the pros do.
00695941 Book/CD Pack.........................$14.95

GUITAR AEROBICS
A 52-WEEK, ONE-LICK-PER-DAY WORKOUT PROGRAM FOR DEVELOPING, IMPROVING & MAINTAINING GUITAR TECHNIQUE
by Troy Nelson
From the former editor of *Guitar One* magazine, here is a daily dose of vitamins to keep your chops fine tuned! Musical styles include rock, blues, jazz, metal, country, and funk. Techniques taught include alternate picking, arpeggios, sweep picking, string skipping, legato, string bending, and rhythm guitar. These exercises will increase speed, and improve dexterity and pick- and fret-hand accuracy. The accompanying CD includes all 365 workout licks plus play-along grooves in every style at eight different metronome settings.
00695946 Book/CD Pack.........................$19.95

GUITAR CLUES
OPERATION PENTATONIC
by Greg Koch
Join renowned guitar master Greg Koch as he clues you in to a wide variety of fun and valuable pentatonic scale applications. Whether you're new to improvising or have been doing it for a while, this book/CD pack will provide loads of delicious licks and tricks that you can use right away, from volume swells and chicken pickin' to intervallic and chordal ideas. The CD includes 65 demo and play-along tracks.
00695827 Book/CD Pack.........................$19.95

INTRODUCTION TO GUITAR TONE & EFFECTS
by David M. Brewster
This book/CD pack teaches the basics of guitar tones and effects, with audio examples on CD. Readers will learn about: overdrive, distortion and fuzz • using equalizers • modulation effects • reverb and delay • multi-effect processors • and more.
00695766 Book/CD Pack.........................$14.95

PICTURE CHORD ENCYCLOPEDIA
This comprehensive guitar chord resource for all playing styles and levels features five voicings of 44 chord qualities for all twelve keys – 2,640 chords in all! For each, there is a clearly illustrated chord frame, as well as *an actual photo* of the chord being played! Includes info on basic fingering principles, open chords and barre chords, partial chords and broken-set forms, and more.
00695224 ....$19.95

SCALE CHORD RELATIONSHIPS
by Michael Mueller & Jeff Schroedl
This book teaches players how to determine which scales to play with which chords, so guitarists will never have to fear chord changes again! This book/CD pack explains how to: recognize keys • analyze chord progressions • use the modes • play over nondiatonic harmony • use harmonic and melodic minor scales • use symmetrical scales such as chromatic, whole-tone and diminished scales • incorporate exotic scales such as Hungarian major and Gypsy minor • and much more!
00695563 Book/CD Pack.........................$14.95

SPEED MECHANICS FOR LEAD GUITAR
Take your playing to the stratosphere with the most advanced lead book by this proven heavy metal author. *Speed Mechanics* is the ultimate technique book for developing the kind of speed and precision in today's explosive playing styles. Learn the fastest ways to achieve speed and control, secrets to make your practice time really count, and how to open your ears and make your musical ideas more solid and tangible. Packed with over 200 vicious exercises including Troy's scorching version of "Flight of the Bumblebee." Music and examples demonstrated on CD. 89-minute audio.
00699323 Book/CD Pack.........................$19.95

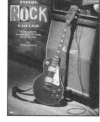

TOTAL ROCK GUITAR
A COMPLETE GUIDE TO LEARNING ROCK GUITAR
by Troy Stetina
This unique and comprehensive source for learning rock guitar is designed to develop both lead and rhythm playing. It covers: getting a tone that rocks • open chords, power chords and barre chords • riffs, scales and licks • string bending, strumming, palm muting, harmonics and alternate picking • all rock styles • and much more. The examples are in standard notation with chord grids and tab, and the CD includes full-band backing for all 22 songs.
00695246 Book/CD Pack.........................$17.95

0308